DATE DUE			
			PRINTED IN U.S.A.

Fantasy and Surrealism

GREAT ARTISTS OF THE WESTERN WORLD

Fantasy and Surrealism

Henri Rousseau

❦

Paul Klee

❦

Marc Chagall

❦

Salvador Dalí

MARSHALL CAVENDISH · LONDON · NEW YORK · SYDNEY

Staff Credits

Editors	Clive Gregory LLB Sue Lyon BA (Honours)	**Picture Researchers**	Vanessa Fletcher BA (Honours) Flavia Howard BA (Honours) Jessica Johnson BA
Art Editors	Chris Legee BFA Kate Sprawson BA (Honours) Keith Vollans LSIAD	**Production Controllers**	Tom Helsby Alan Stewart BSc
Deputy Editor	John Kirkwood BSc (Honours)	**Secretary**	Lynn Smail
Sub-editors	Caroline Bugler BA (Honours), MA Sue Churchill BA (Honours) Alison Cole BA, MPhil Jenny Mohammadi Nigel Rodgers BA (Honours), MA Penny Smith Will Steeds BA (Honours), MA	**Editorial Director** **Publishing Manager** **Managing Editor**	Maggi McCormick Robert Paulley BSc Alan Ross BA (Honours)
Designers	Stuart John Julie Stanniland	**Consultant and Authenticator**	Sharon Fermor BA (Honours) Lecturer in the Extra-Mural Department of London University and Lecturer in Art History at Sussex University

Reference Edition Published 1988

Published by Marshall Cavendish Corporation
147 West Merrick Road
Freeport, Long Island
N.Y. 11520

Typeset by Litho Link Ltd., Welshpool
Printed and Bound by Dai Nippon
Printing Co., Hong Kong Ltd.

All rights reserved. No part of this book may be reproduced or utilized in any form or by any means electronic or mechanical including photocopying, recording, or by an information storage and retrieval system, without permission from the copyright holder.

© Marshall Cavendish Limited MCMLXXXV,
MCMLXXXVIII

Library of Congress Cataloging-in-Publication Data

Main entry under title:

Great Artists of the Western World II.

Includes index.
1. Artists – Biography. I. Marshall Cavendish Corporation.
N40.G774 1988   709'.2'2 [B]   88–4317
ISBN 0–86307–900–8 (set)

ISBN 0–86307–900–8 (set)
        0–86307–759–5 (vol)

Preface

Looking at pictures can be one of the greatest pleasures that life has to offer. Note, however, those two words 'can be'; all too many of us remember all too clearly those grim afternoons of childhood when we were dragged, bored to tears and complaining bitterly, through room after room of Italian primitives by well-meaning relations or tight-lipped teachers. It was enough to put one off pictures for life – which, for some of us, was exactly what it did.

For if gallery-going is to be the fun it should be, certain conditions must be fulfilled. First, the pictures we are to see must be good pictures. Not necessarily great pictures – even a few of these can be daunting, while too many at a time may prove dangerously indigestible. But they must be well-painted, by good artists who know precisely both the effect they want to achieve and how best to achieve it. Second, we must limit ourselves as to quantity. Three rooms – four at the most – of the average gallery are more than enough for one day, and for best results we should always leave while we are still fresh, well before satiety sets in. Now I am well aware that this is a counsel of perfection: sometimes, in the case of a visiting exhibition or, perhaps, when we are in a foreign city with only a day to spare, we shall have no choice but to grit our teeth and stagger on to the end. But we shall not enjoy ourselves quite so much, nor will the pictures remain so long or so clearly in our memory.

The third condition is all-important: we must know something about the painters whose work we are looking at. And this is where this magnificent series of volumes – one of which you now hold in your hands – can make all the difference. No painting is an island: it must, if it is to be worth a moment's attention, express something of the personality of its painter. And that painter, however individual a genius, cannot but reflect the country, style and period, together with the views and attitudes of the people among whom he or she was born and bred. Even a superficial understanding of these things will illuminate a painting for us far better than any number of spotlights, and if in addition we have learnt something about the artist as a person – life and loves, character and beliefs, friends and patrons, and the places to which he or she travelled – the interest and pleasure that the work will give us will be multiplied a hundredfold.

Great Artists of the Western World will provide you with just such an insight into the life and work of some of the outstanding painters of Europe and America. The text is informative without ever becoming dry or academic, not limiting itself to the usual potted biographies but forever branching out into the contemporary world outside and beyond workshop or studio. The illustrations, in colour throughout, have been dispensed in almost reckless profusion. For those who, like me, revel in playing the Attribution Game – the object of which is to guess the painter of each picture before allowing one's eye to drop to the label – the little sections on 'Trademarks' are a particularly happy feature; but every aficionado will have particular preferences, and I doubt whether there is an art historian alive, however distinguished, who would not find some fascinating nugget of previously unknown information among the pages that follow.

This series, however, is not intended for art historians. It is designed for ordinary people like you and me – and for our older children – who are fully aware that the art galleries of the world constitute a virtually bottomless mine of potential enjoyment, and who are determined to extract as much benefit and advantage from it as they possibly can. All the volumes in this collection will enable us to do just that, expanding our knowledge not only of art itself but also of history, religion, mythology, philosophy, fashion, interior decoration, social customs and a thousand other subjects as well. So let us not simply leave them around, flipping idly through a few of their pages once in a while. Let us read them as they deserve to be read – and welcome a new dimension in our lives.

John Julius Norwich

John Julius Norwich is a writer and broadcaster who has written histories of Venice and of Norman Sicily as well as several works on history, art and architecture. He has also made over twenty documentary films for television, including the recent Treasure Houses of Britain series which was widely acclaimed after repeated showings in the United States.

Lord Norwich is Chairman of the Venice in Peril Fund, and member of the Executive Committee of the British National Trust, an independently funded body established for the protection of places of historic interest and natural beauty.

Contents

Introduction

The rise of Modernist painting in the early years of the 20th century in turn brought forth a variety of new artistic movements, aimed at providing an alternative set of values and aspirations for the artists of the avant-garde. In the main, these new trends were marked by a rejection of naturalism and a desire to replace it with the exploration of a more fundamental reality: that of Man's inner nature. In pursuing this goal, many painters found inspiration in the most basic art forms, namely primitive, folk and naive art.

The Innocent Eye

Even though he was indisputably the greatest of the naive painters, it is probably fair to suggest that Rousseau's work would not have created quite the same impact in any other period in art history. The simplifications which were forced on him by his own limited technique were mirrored in the experiments of other progressive artists. Gauguin, for example, had used flattened, highly coloured shapes and taken liberties with the laws of perspective while, in his later works, Seurat had employed sharply silhouetted figures that were reminiscent of Rousseau's naive cut-outs. Rousseau had met or exhibited with both these artists and doubtless felt that he was in the same tradition.

In the following decade, Rousseau also attracted the attention of Picasso, at a time when the Spaniard was developing an interest in African carvings. For Picasso and the Cubists, these primitive sculptures exuded a raw energy that centuries of civilization had stripped away from European art and it is easy to see how this viewpoint could be complemented by an appreciation of the pictures of Rousseau, whose lack of sophistication seemed to imply a rejection of the achievements of Western culture.

The appeal of the primitive and the naive for the Cubists was primarily visual but, for subsequent art movements, there were other considerations.

Philippe Halsman/John Hillelson Agency

Felix Klee/COSMOPRESS, Geneva 1988

H. Roger Viollet

The Dadaists admired naive painting for its apparent denial of both talent and style, and some reflection of this can be found in Klee's deliberate attempts to emulate the simplicity of children's art (for example, p.50). For the Surrealists, meanwhile, it was the uncluttered thought processes of the child that were of importance (rather than the actual pictures which they produced). A child's mind could provide the key to the imagination and the unconscious since, as Breton argued in his Manifesto of Surrealism (1924), 'childhood is the nearest state to true life'.

However, Rousseau was not hailed as a forerunner of Surrealism purely because of his childlike vision; he also anticipated some of the most characteristic features of the movement. The unsettling effect created by a distorted sense of scale was a favourite device of Surrealists such as

National Gallery, Prague

Magritte and this was prefigured in Rousseau's works by the huge, hallucinatory plant forms that dominated his jungle scenes (pp.19, 34-5) and were to inspire the fantastic landscapes of Max Ernst. In addition, Rousseau frequently achieved a mood of dream-like irrationality, in which seemingly incompatible objects were brought together.

During his lifetime, Rousseau's art was championed by the French poet and critic, Guillaume Apollinaire. The latter's interests extended far beyond the compass of naive painting, however, and affected many developments in modern art. In 1913, he published The Cubist Painters, a celebration of his friendship with Picasso and his circle, and he was particularly drawn to the colouristic form of the style, known as 'Orphism', a term which he coined to describe the work of Robert Delaunay (see p.78). It was Apollinaire, too, who invented the word 'Surrealism', using it twice in 1917, in the programme for the ballet Parade and in the preface to his play, The Breasts of Tiresias. Seven years later, Breton was radically to transform the meaning of this term in his Manifesto (p.110) but, in its original sense – where it suggested 'lyrical fantasy' – Apollinaire's term could certainly be applied to the art of Chagall.

The artists
(above) Rousseau in a detail from Myself: Portrait-Landscape. *(opposite, clockwise) Dalí in a photograph by Philippe Halsman; Chagall aged about 30; Klee in about 1911.*

Inspiration from Russia
Chagall's work bridged a number of styles without conforming to any single School. From the Cubists, and particularly the Orphists, he derived much of his fragmented compositional technique (for example, pp.85 and 86), although Chagall found their attachment to the physical world too limiting and he soon learnt to dispense with their angular, faceted forms. Similarly, his taste for juxtaposing seemingly unconnected motifs (pp.83, 87) has given rise to comparisons with the Surrealists.

Like many of his contemporaries, Chagall sought inspiration from simple, anti-naturalistic sources. In his case, however, these sources were not to be found in ethnic or naive art, but in the popular culture of his native Russia. He frequently used the format of icons, for example, where the force of a large, central image was amplified by a series of smaller, episodic details. Chagall did not restrict this approach to religious subjects like The White Crucifixion, but also employed it in secular works like The Fiddler (p. 83), where the typically Russian musician was surrounded by tiny features

Photo: Carmelo Guadagno/The Solomon R. Guggenheim Museum, New York

Naive composition
(left) In The Artillerymen *(1893), Rousseau deliberately arranges his subjects so that they resemble toy soldiers. And his childlike composition is further emphasized by the flat forms and the alternating light and dark colours.*

which evoked memories of the artist's homeland.

Chagall also drew extensively on Russian lubok (popular woodblock prints). From these, he derived not only some of his most characteristic images – such as the wandering Jew in Over Vitebsk (pp.88-9) and The White Crucifixion – but also the air of stylized innocence which he infuzed into so many of his paintings. Folk art, like primitive art, found many new devotees during the Modernist period and it is notable that Russian prints were illustrated in the important Almanac produced by the Blaue Reiter group in 1912.

A World of Fantasy
Klee was also associated with this avant-garde body, contributing seventeen drawings to its second exhibition. His point of contact with the circle was through his close friend, Franz Marc, with whom he shared a passing interest in Orphic Cubism (most evident in Full Moon, p.58), although in the long term the example of Kandinsky's subjectless paintings was probably more important for Klee.

In common with Chagall, Klee had affinities with several movements while belonging to none. One such affinity was with the Dada group, which flourished briefly between 1915 and 1923 and which effectively provided an artistic prologue to Surrealism. The Dadaists adopted an iconoclastic stance, denying the value of aesthetics or reason in the realms of art. The result was a series of absurd fantasies, typified by the nonsensical, imaginary machines designed by Francis Picabia. Klee's whimsical Twittering Machine (p.59) was a clear reflection of this trend.

The Dada movement soon burnt itself out, but its love of the irrational was preserved in Surrealism. From the start, Breton defined the latter as 'a kind of psychic automatism' and urged artists to use the chance discoveries made by automatic drawings (that is, drawings produced very rapidly and without prior planning) as a means of unlocking the secrets of the unconscious mind. Breton's intention, here, was to devize a pictorial equivalent to Freud's 'free association' techniques (see p.70).

Klee certainly experimented with automatism and it was probably for this reason that he was invited to contribute to the first Surrealist exhibition. However, he maintained a wary distance from the theories of the movement and was reluctant to surrender control of his art to the workings of his subconscious. Automatism, for him, provided only the initial spark for works that were ultimately both ordered and regulated.

Surrealistic Dreams
In Dalí, however, Breton found a much more willing disciple for his ideas. As a young man, the Spaniard filled his first Surrealist canvases with the full range of Freudian sexual imagery, linking his obsessive desires with fears of castration, impotence and female dominance.

Dalí was also very much taken with the 'psycho-pathological' theories of the Surrealists, through which a special significance was read into the paintings of visionaries, mediums and the mentally sick (the idea being that members of any of these categories would compose pictures quite independently of the normal thought processes). Dalí's infamous 'paranoiac-critical' method developed out of the third of these categories, as the artist strove to imitate the mental disorder which caused the sufferer to interpret real objects or events in an irrational fashion.

The hallmark of this 'method' was the double image, where Dalí sought to startle his spectators with surprising transformations of natural phenomena. The most celebrated instance of this is The Metamorphosis of Narcissus (pp.122-3), but Dalí extended the technique to include other, individual motifs from his repertoire. Thus, the obscene, mouthless self-portrait which figured prominently in The Persistence of Memory (pp.120-21) was based on a rock formation at Cadaqués where the Dalí family owned a home.

Dalí's striking imagery was enhanced by the rigorous trompe l'oeil style which he employed. This feature – which he shared with artists like Magritte and Delvaux – was aimed at bringing a fantastic quality into his pictures, imbuing them with the vivid and irrational clarity of a dream.

Dalí's break with the Surrealists occurred at the end of the 1930s and was hastened by his failure to dissociate himself from Fascism. The movement itself held its final exhibition in 1947 and officially came to an end with Breton's death in 1966. Long before this, however, the real impetus of Surrealism had passed into other art forms. The lessons of automatism were taken up by Jackson Pollock and the Abstract Expressionists, while the possibilities of an irrational, trompe l'oeil approach were to prove a major source of inspiration for both the Photorealists and the Pop artists.

Rousseau/Myself: Portrait-Landscape/National Gallery, Prague

HENRI ROUSSEAU
1844-1910

The most famous of all naive artists, Henri Rousseau spent his working life as a customs official manning the Parisian toll gates. He began painting in his spare time, but took early retirement as soon as he could to devote himself to art. Rousseau's unwavering faith in his own abilities enabled him to endure great financial hardship and the ridicule of a public that found his art both comical and incomprehensible.

Rousseau's ambition was to paint in the correct academic style, but, by a strange irony, he found his work was valued not by the traditionalists, but by a small circle of avant-garde intellectuals and artists that included Gauguin and Picasso. They admired the total innocence and charm of his character and art, and it is for these reasons that Rousseau is more highly regarded today than the academic painters he sought to emulate.

A True Innocent

An undistinguished customs official, Rousseau was supremely sure of his artistic talent and had a childlike innocence which endeared him to the Bohemian writers and artists of the Parisian avant-garde.

Henri Rousseau, France's eccentric naive painter, was born in a medieval tower in the provincial town of Laval in north-western France on 21 May 1844. His father Julien ran an ironmonger's shop on the ground floor of the tower until bankruptcy forced him out of the trade. Neither Julien nor his wife were the slightest bit interested in art, and Rousseau was later to lament their indifference to painting and their poverty which had deprived him of the artistic education to which he felt his genius entitled him.

Yet the records of Rousseau's school career hardly suggest that he was a child prodigy – he failed most of his exams, and showed interest only in music, poetry and drawing. By the time he was 19, Rousseau's lack of academic distinction had consigned him to a dreary job as a clerk in a local lawyer's office, but this ended after only a few months when he was found guilty of stealing stamps worth 25 francs from his employer.

Following his trial and one month's im-

The young Rousseau
(above) A short man with chestnut hair, Rousseau had modest aspirations, but longed for bourgeois respectability.

Artistic inspiration
(above right and right) Although Rousseau claimed he was inspired by the luxuriant plant life of the Mexican jungle, in reality he never went there. Instead, his imagination must have been fired by his visits to the botanical gardens in Paris.

An unusual birthplace
(left) Rousseau was born in a medieval tower called the Beucheresse Gate, part of Laval's fortified wall. The family home – the right-hand tower next to the gateway through which woodcutters had once passed on their way from the town to the nearby forest – was an appropriate birthplace for an aspiring artist who spent most of his working life manning the toll-gates of Paris while dreaming of trees and jungles.

prisonment, Rousseau enlisted with the 51st Infantry, hoping to win back his parents' esteem. The artist was later to embellish his undistinguished army career by claiming that he had been sent to Mexico as a clarinettist during Napoleon III's campaign in support of the Emperor Maximilian. But his lyrical descriptions of the Mexican jungle were in reality nothing more than an elaborate fantasy that fell apart when he was closely questioned. Nor is there any evidence to support Rousseau's assertion that he played a heroic part in the defence of the town of Dreux against the Germans in 1870.

DOMESTIC HAPPINESS

When Rousseau left the army in 1868 he moved to Paris, where he soon met and fell in love with Clémence Boitard, the seamstress daughter of his landlady. The artist felt a constant and overwhelming need for love and companionship, and marriage to Clémence gave him the happiest 20 years of his life, although the couple had more than their fair share of misfortune – five of their seven children died of tuberculosis in childhood.

In 1871, Rousseau started working for the Paris Customs Office. At that time taxes were levied on

The Toll House
(right) From 1871, Rousseau worked as a customs officer on the Paris toll-gates. He was given all the easy tasks and drew and painted in his spare time.

Courtauld Institute Galleries (Courtauld Collection)

certain commodities such as salt, wine, milk and grain, and it was Rousseau's job to stand at the city toll-gates to check carts for smuggled goods. The work was not very demanding, and it left him with plenty of time to contemplate nature in the leafy suburbs where he worked. He began to draw and paint in his spare time and days off. His supervisors seem to have been very indulgent, and they assigned him all the easy tasks at the toll-house, although whether this was in recognition of his artistic talent and need to paint, as Rousseau thought, or because he was unable to cope with anything difficult, is a matter of opinion. At any rate, Rousseau was never promoted to the rank of 'Douanier' (Customs Officer) that his nick-name of 'Douanier Rousseau' implies.

FRIENDLY ADVICE

Rousseau's naivety – coupled with his utterly unshakeable belief in his own artistic abilities – meant that he was not at all afraid of approaching the artists he most admired for their opinions on his work. The painter Clément, who lived in the neighbourhood, gave him some well-meaning advice and helped him obtain a copyist's card giving access to the Louvre and other galleries on study days. His great idol, Gérôme, wisely told him to study nature closely and preserve his naive style. While it was Rousseau's dearest wish to paint in the correct manner taught 'by the

F. Jalain/Explorer

Portrait of a Woman/Musée d'Orsay, Paris

A portrait-landscape
(above) One of Rousseau's unusual portraits with a landscape background, this painting probably shows his first wife, Clémence, to whom he was devoted. On Sundays they would go to the Bois de Boulogne or the forests around Paris, visit the races at Longchamps or the Botanical Gardens with its hot-houses and zoo. When Clémence died in 1888, Rousseau mourned 'a pure, sacred union of living only for another'.

Academy, both Clément and Gérôme realized that the uniqueness of his vision came precisely from the fact that he was self-taught.

Rousseau made his public debut as an artist in 1885 when he sent two pictures to the Salon des Artistes Indépendants, an exhibiting society set up by avant-garde artists who were unable to get their work accepted at the Salon des Artistes Français. Rousseau's paintings were received with a mixture of incomprehension and mirth. One critic wrote, 'His paintings resemble the daubings that delighted us when we were six. I spent an hour in front of these masterpieces, scrutinizing the faces of the visitors. There wasn't one who didn't laugh till tears came. Happy Rousseau!'

Undeterred by the hostile reception, Rousseau continued to exhibit his work every year at the Indépendants, where it hung alongside pictures by Seurat, Redon and Signac. The mockery

The exciting World's Fair
(above) The World's Fair not only provided Rousseau with material for his paintings, it also inspired him to write a comedy – performed for the first time in 1968.

continued, and at one stage reached such epic proportions that the Indépendants talked about dropping Rousseau as a member of their group. At the meeting when the matter of the embarrassing anonymous member was discussed, Rousseau's case was defended by Toulouse-Lautrec, while Rousseau, quite unaware that he was the subject of the debate, argued fervently in favour of his own expulsion.

A TIMELY DIVERSION

In 1888, his wife Clémence died from tuberculosis, leaving Rousseau a grief-stricken widower with two children to look after. Fortunately, a new source of enthusiasm and interest entered his life the following year, when the World's Fair opened in Paris. In a series of glass pavilions at the foot of the newly erected Eiffel Tower, Rousseau was able to see a reconstructed Mexican palace, African and Asian villages, and all the paraphernalia of faraway lands and exotic cultures brought together in one place. He viewed it all with intense curiosity and total lack of discrimination, gathering together a wealth of visual material that was to find its outlet in his allegorical paintings and jungle pictures. So inspired was he by the experience that he even wrote a three-act comedy entitled *A Visit to the Exhibition of 1889*, which the Comédie Française politely rejected on the grounds that it would be too expensive to produce.

Shortly after the exhibition closed, Rousseau showed at the Indépendants *Myself: Portrait-Landscape* (p.11), in which he appeared in his official uniform sporting a Rembrandt-like beret, holding a palette, and standing by a toll-house on

the Seine. It was Rousseau's definitive statement that he was an artist, and it was greeted with torrents of abuse. One critic sarcastically remarked, 'The portrait-landscape is his own invention and I would advise him to take out a patent on it as unscrupulous characters are quite capable of using it.' Blissfully unaware of the irony, Rousseau took this as a compliment, and cut out the review to paste into the scrapbook where he kept all his press notices, good and bad. He was to call himself 'the inventor of the portrait-landscape' for the rest of his life.

Rousseau took early retirement from the Customs Office in 1893 to devote himself entirely to his art. His pension was rather meagre, and he sometimes had to supplement it by playing his violin in the streets and by paying his bills with paintings rather than money. His two rather neglected children, malnourished and tired of

their father's unconventional lifestyle, were sent to stay with relatives in Angers.

It was around this time that Rousseau found his paintings were being taken seriously by the Parisian avant-garde. He struck up a bizarre friendship with the writer Alfred Jarry, 30 years younger than himself, but also a native of Laval, who began to act as his publicist. Jarry introduced Rousseau to new intellectual circles, gave him his nick-name 'Douanier', and commissioned him to do an illustration for his new magazine. The retired customs official soon found himself attending Gauguin's Saturday *soirées* and mixing with people like Degas, Strindberg and Mallarmé. He was so impressed with these gatherings that he began to hold his own 'artistic and literary evenings' in his studio, to which he invited a curious mixture of friends, students, local shopkeepers and progressive artists and writers.

Rousseau's Brilliant Publicist

Around 1893, Rousseau formed an unlikely friendship with Alfred Jarry, a poet and playwright, who was later to achieve fame as the creator of the absurd drama *Ubu Roi*. The naive painter of 50 and the brilliant young man of 20 had little in common apart from the fact that they were both natives of Laval, and that Jarry's father had been at school with Rousseau, nor are the precise details of their meeting known. However, the unconventional Jarry was greatly impressed with Rousseau's originality, and he did what he could to obtain favourable publicity for him. In return, Rousseau invited Jarry to stay in his studio when he was evicted from his lodgings in 1897. He also painted a portrait of the dramatist showing him with two owls and a pet chameleon, but this was unfortunately destroyed by Jarry's frequent use of it as a target in revolver practice and no photographic record of it survives.

H. Roger Viollet.

Bulloz

Musée d'Orsay, Paris

An intellectual friend
(above) Jarry frequented the circle connected with the newspaper Mercure de France, *and introduced Rousseau to Parisian intellectuals.*

War (1894)
(left) His association with Jarry gave Rousseau new impetus and assurance. This striking painting evolved from a lithograph commissioned by Jarry for his magazine L'Ymagier. *The painting prompted the only article of any length which praised Rousseau during his lifetime, written, at Jarry's suggestion, for* **Mercure de France.**

won the Legion of Honour, although this episode did not end quite so happily as the artist burst into tears at the local police station when he found out that he had been the victim of a hoax.

The banquet that Picasso held in Rousseau's honour in 1908 also contained a strong element of parody. Prominent intellectuals and artists assembled in Picasso's studio beneath a ceiling festooned with streamers proclaiming Rousseau's fame. The food ordered from the caterers never seemed to arrive (Picasso had got the day wrong), but the party's spirits were maintained by 50 bottles of wine, rowdy jokes and songs. As the poet Apollinaire recited his poem praising the 'Glorious painter of our dear Republic', Rousseau, sitting on his makeshift throne of packing cases,

Homage to Rousseau

(above) In 1908, Picasso held an improvised banquet at his Bateau-Lavoir studio in Montmartre to celebrate his purchase of one of Rousseau's portraits, which he had bought in a junk shop for five francs. The painting was hung on the studio wall and members of the avant-garde gathered beneath Chinese lanterns, garlands and flags for an entertaining evening in honour of their friend.

A proud artist

(right) This photograph shows Rousseau in his studio, in front of The Merry Jesters *(p.30). He had always believed in his own talent and remained impervious to the public ridicule which often greeted his work.*

Elaborate programmes designed with coloured inks announced the order of the entertainments, which invariably included Rousseau's tearful rendition of his waltz 'Clémence' on his violin in front of a portrait of his first wife.

Rousseau's new friends found his extreme innocence an endless source of amusement. Gauguin once persuaded him that the President of France had invited him to a grand reception at the Elysée Palace, and Rousseau, not thinking this in any way unusual, turned up to the event full of expectation only to be sent away. Yet he had the wit to tell his friends that the President of France himself had met him at the gate and explained that he could not be admitted because he was not wearing evening dress. There was also the occasion when someone told Rousseau that he had

felt that the artistic recognition he had waited for all his life had finally arrived. He didn't even mind the molten wax that was dripping on to his head from the Chinese lantern above.

During these years, Rousseau was kept constantly busy with portrait commissions from the people in his neighbourhood, and with teaching; he had begun to take on private students as it was his cherished wish to found an Academy of his own. Yet his financial problems were as acute as ever, and the pitiful begging letters he sent to friends – 'If you could just lend me 20 or 30 francs you would make me very happy. Right now I have 20 centimes in my possession' – reveal how perilously close to destitution he came.

In 1907, he was arrested for fraud and embezzlement, although this was more the result

A poet friend

It was probably Jarry who introduced Guillaume Apollinaire to Rousseau in 1906, and the young poet quickly took over the role of Rousseau's champion and defender following Jarry's death in 1907. The ageing painter was so impressed with his illustrious new friend that he used a special notebook to keep a record of their appointments, and painted a portrait of him together with his mistress, the artist Marie Laurencin, in the guise of a muse, in homage to his poetic gift. Apollinaire introduced Rousseau to many leading avant-garde artists, including Picasso and Delaunay, and he composed several poems in Rousseau's honour both during the artist's lifetime and after his death, the most famous of which is the epitaph that decorates his tombstone (below).

> Gentle Rousseau you can hear us
> We salute you
> Delaunay his wife Monsieur Queval and myself
> Let our luggage pass duty-free through the gate of heaven
> We are bringing you brushes paints and canvas
> That you may spend your sacred leisure hours
> Painting in the light of truth eternal
> As you once painted my portrait
> Facing the stars.

Colorphoto Hinz

The Muse Inspiring the Poet/Kunstmuseum, Basel

The Muse Inspiring the Poet
(above) This double portrait shows Rousseau's friend Apollinaire with his mistress, Marie Laurencin.

Rousseau's tomb
(right) In 1911 friends arranged a proper tomb for Rousseau's remains, which were moved to Laval in 1947.

Edimage

of his incredible naivety than any criminal intention. An acquaintance had asked him to open a bank account in a false name in order to obtain money, and Rousseau, who never suspected anybody of evil motives, was happy to oblige. In the end it was his obvious simplicity that saved him at the trial. His paintings were shown in the courtroom as evidence of his 'primitive' mentality, and his defence argued that the jury should spare him because he had the mental outlook of a child. As the lawyer concluded his speech, Rousseau shouted out 'Well, now you've finished can I go?' Everyone was so amused and disarmed that he was given a suspended sentence.

The little money that Rousseau did have during his last years he spent on donations to the poor and sick and on gifts to his last love, Léonie.

Rousseau's second wife Joséphine had died in 1903 after only four years of marriage, and the artist was convinced that Léonie, an ugly widow of 57 who worked in a shop, was destined to become his third. However, neither the certificates of honesty and talent that he obtained from his friends, nor the will he made out leaving all his worldly possessions to her, could break down Léonie's resistance to the marriage.

Shortly after his last amorous disappointment, Rousseau fell seriously ill. An untreated leg wound turned gangrenous, and he died in hospital on 2 September 1910. The artist was buried in an obscure pauper's grave at the Bagneaux cemetery in Paris, yet only a month after his death obituary notices were comparing him to the Renaissance master Uccello.

Childlike Dreams

Rousseau's unique vision was inspired by his love of nature and by his private fantasy world, which was fuelled by his visits to the Paris botanical gardens and by a book on wild beasts.

Rousseau once confided to a friend: 'Nothing makes me happier than to contemplate nature and to paint it. Would you believe that when I go out in the country and see all that sun, all that greenery, and all those flowers, I sometimes say to myself: All that belongs to me, it does!' Love of nature, and the desire to possess it, was what prompted Rousseau's first hesitant steps in art. The few drawings of his that survive (most were torn to shreds after his death by his family) show the enormous pleasure he took in delineating trees with their soaring trunks and leaves shivering in the breeze, and the blades of grass at their feet.

Rousseau drew the initial inspiration for his landscapes from the suburbs where he worked, and from the Sunday outings he made to the forests around Paris. In his vision, these quiet, almost dull scenes were transformed into an innocent Eden, although it was a modern paradise in which factory chimneys, balloons, dirigibles and football players all had their place. The pictures all give the feeling of having been painted at one remove from the scenes they depict, and this may be partly because, although Rousseau was in the habit of sketching out-of-doors, he preferred instead to work up his landscapes in the studio afterwards.

The Jardin des Plantes in Paris, with its glasshouses full of majestic palms and camelias, stimulated his imagination in another way and set him dreaming of faraway lands. As Rousseau later

The Sunday painter
(right) Rousseau began his artistic career as a Sunday painter, recording the leafy landscape of the Parisian suburbs. This delightful picture reveals his lack of formal training in the clumsy perspective – which he never mastered – and in the rather awkward figure-style.

Edimedia

The Painter and his Model/Nina Kandinsky Collection, Paris

Nature studies
(left) Very few of Rousseau's drawings have survived, but this delicate ink study shows how scrupulously he observed nature. His friend, the poet Apollinaire, described how Rousseau 'would wander around Paris to gather a profusion of leaves, which he would then copy'.

The Vase of Flowers/Albright Knox Art Gallery, Buffalo, New York

remarked, 'When I enter these hot-houses and see these strange plants from exotic countries, I feel as if I have stepped into a dream.' In his famous jungle pictures, he isolated the individual flowers and leaves of his favourite plants and blew them up to an enormous size, giving equal emphasis to every detail, to create a fictional jungle that resembled the 'Mexico of his youth' (which seems to have existed only in his imagination).

STRIVING FOR NATURALISM

Rousseau once claimed that he had 'no master but nature', and the landscape elements in his paintings are always the most assured. Perhaps it was his close study of the natural world that led him to describe himself as a 'realist painter' in an autobiographical sketch, even though his paintings often inhabit a world of fantasy and are painted with an almost childlike naivety. At the core of Rousseau's work lies the strange paradox that, while his dearest wish was to paint in the precise, realistic style of the Academician Gérôme, his laborious efforts towards that end resulted in an odd parody of the conventions of academic painting. It was the progressive artists of the avant-garde who most appreciated Rousseau's original manner, but he was often indifferent to their work, finding it too 'unfinished' for his taste. Yet, in his own way, Rousseau had arrived at a similar position in painting to them.

Colourful bouquets
(left) Around 1890, Rousseau began to paint small flower pictures, freely indulging his love of bold pattern and colour. He often chose individual flowers for their symbolic meaning and enlivened the displays with stylized leaves and sprigs of mimosa.

Fact and fantasy
(right and above right) In the last years, Rousseau painted his famous jungle scenes, revelling in the luxuriant landscapes of his dreams. Inspired by the exotic plants he saw in the hot-houses of the Botanical Gardens, he began by drawing their outlines on to the canvas and then very carefully colouring them in. For the strange animals and figures that appear in his compositions, he looked through the photos in a children's album of wild beasts (above right) for material to copy.

Colorphoto Hinz

Edimage

Photograph of jaguar from 'Bêtes Sauvages'

Negro attacked by a Jaguar/Kunstmuseum, Basel

In Rousseau's pictures, conventional laws of perspective, proportion and illumination, which are the traditional means by which artists create an illusion of reality, are either flouted or ignored. Because he was self-taught, Rousseau found it extremely difficult to master some of the complicated technical aspects of painting, and developed various means of trying to avoid them. Perspective posed the worst problem, but the profusion of luxuriant vegetation in the later pictures was a convenient way out of having to create an impression of recession into depth. Rousseau also found that the difficulty of painting feet (hard to do because they involve so many different spatial planes) could be circumvented by placing his characters ankle-deep in grass.

The artist found it hardest of all to paint faces, and the thickness of the paint on some of his portraits points to the way in which he was forced to make constant revisions. In an attempt to create an accurate likeness, Rousseau, in a rather bizarre procedure, measured the eyes, noses and mouths of his sitters with the end of his paintbrush and transferred the exact measurements onto the canvas, taking no account whatsoever of foreshortening. To get the flesh tones right, he held up tubes of paint or his loaded paintbrush against the sitter's face. Needless to say, this dedicated pursuit of realism resulted in a very unnaturalistic image of the person, but the portraits do have an immediacy and presence that is amplified by Rousseau's choice of peculiarly

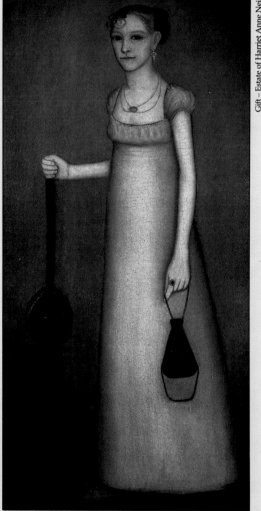

Gift – Estate of Harriet Anne Neil

COMPARISONS

Naive Painters

Naive painting has always existed as a form of folk art, but it is only really since the beginning of the 20th century that it has been thought worthy of critical appraisal, and its qualities of charm and freshness have become highly valued. True naive artists are self-taught and paint the world as they see it in a simplified and idiosyncratic style, taking no account of the laws of perspective, proportion and foreshortening. Naive painters nearly always use colour in an unscientific manner, and show a strong preference for bright, vibrant tones, which sometimes bear little relation to colours in nature.

Bridgeman Art Library

Private Collection

Fogg Art Museum, Harvard University

Hanny Lüthi (1919-1982) Sacré Coeur
(left) Hanny Lüthi painted as a hobby all her life, executing minutely detailed compositions in bold, vivid colours.

Ammi Phillips (1788-1865) Harriet Leavens
(above) Part of the charm of this early 19th-century portrait exists in its two-dimensionality.

Memories of Mexico
(above) Rousseau led many of his friends to believe that his tropical landscapes were inspired by the Mexico jungle, which he claimed to have seen on his 'military campaigns'. In a drunken tribute to the painter, Apollinaire recited the following poem, composed in his honour: 'Do you recall, Rousseau, the Aztec landscape, the forests of mango and pineapple trees, monkeys spilling the blood of watermelons and the blond emperor who was shot down there. The paintings you do – you saw them in Mexico, a red sun decorated the banana bushes . . .'

Tropical Forest with Monkeys/National Gallery of Art, Washington/John Hay Whitney Collection   Detail: Tropical Forest with Monkeys

appropriate accessories and invented landscape backgrounds (p.11)

Rousseau admired the animal paintings of Delacroix and Gérôme, but he did not directly copy them in his own work. He had a far more convenient source of ready-made images in a book he owned, published by the department store Galeries Lafayette and entitled *Wild Beasts.* The 200 photographs in this book, which were mainly taken in the Paris zoo, enabled the artist to observe the movements of lions about to spring on their prey and monkeys hanging from trees, and place them in a fictional jungle of his own imagining. Rousseau used a pantograph, or mechanical enlarger, to help him trace the outline of the animal onto the canvas, and then proceeded to painstakingly colour it in.

A FEELING FOR COLOUR

The artist's greatest strength lay in his intuitive feel for colour, and the beautiful patterns it formed across the canvas. Rousseau always prided himself on the variety of tones he was able to introduce into each picture, and one visitor to his studio heard him proclaim with pleasure that he was on to his 22nd shade of green. He often worked on all the related shades in a picture at once, covering every inch of the picture space with meticulous thoroughness. Rousseau's methods may have been unconventional, but they succeeded in creating an impression of great chromatic richness. It is the colours, above all, that suggest the mood of his pictures, which vary from calm and repose to haunting mystery and menace.

Monkey business
(above) Rousseau was especially fond of monkeys and enjoyed watching their antics at the Paris zoo. In his album, too, he read about how the gibbon apes (seen here) were 'incomparably superior to acrobats'.

TRADEMARKS

Tropical Plants

The dense vegetation in Rousseau's imaginary jungles consists of his favourite plants, leaves and flowers magnified to an enormous size to create an impression of luxuriance.

The Sleeping Gypsy

On 10 July 1898, Rousseau wrote to the Mayor of Laval offering to sell *The Sleeping Gypsy* to the town, as 'a souvenir of one of its children'. The Mayor turned down the proposal, but Rousseau's letter to him provides an interesting explanation of the painting in the artist's own words. Rousseau saw the picture as a 'realistic' work in the popular Oriental mode: 'A wandering Negress, playing the mandolin, with a jar at her side (a vase containing drinking water), sleeps profoundly, exhausted. A lion happens to come by, sniffs her, but doesn't devour her. The moonlight is very poetic. The scene takes place in a completely arid desert. The Gypsy wears Oriental garb.' Unfortunately, this haunting masterpiece went unrecognized in Rousseau's lifetime. It was discovered in 1923, in a plumber's workshop in Paris.

51" × 6' 7"/oil on canvas/Gift of Mrs Simon Guggenheim

Louis Matout/Boghari Woman killed by a Lioness/Musée Municipal des Ursulines, Mâcon

Intuitive colour sense
(below) Rousseau's use of subtle rainbow colours and instinctive love of chromatic harmonies, links him with many of the abstract painters of the 20th century.

Oriental drama
(above) Rousseau had seen Louis Matout's painting and seems to have been fascinated by its theme. But in his own version, 'the feline, although ferocious, is reluctant to leap upon its prey'.

Mandolin and scrapbook
(right) Much of Rousseau's source material has been found among his belongings.

Collection, The Museum of Modern Art, New York

'What peace! Mystery believes it is all alone and it strips itself naked.'

Jean Cocteau

Mysterious encounter
(above) The juxtaposition of the slumbering gypsy and the immobile lion – which seems to belong to the world of a twilight mirage – gives the painting a dreamlike quality which was greatly admired by the Surrealists.

Layton Art Collection/Milwaukee Art Museum

Academic inspiration
(left) Rousseau strove to imitate the accomplished, academic style of Gérôme and he borrowed The Sleeping Gypsy's *desert setting from Gérôme's magnificent* Two Majesties.

Gallery

Rousseau is deservedly regarded as the greatest of all naive painters; his boldness and originality of vision were second to none and he maintained his beguiling sense of freshness even when painting large and elaborate compositions. His imaginative richness comes out particularly in his jungle scenes, which vary greatly in mood, from the stormy drama of Surprised! to the trance-like stillness of The Snake Charmer, and from the bizarre humour of The Merry Jesters to the fairytale fantasy of The Dream.

His other works included some remarkably arresting portraits, such as Portrait of a Woman and Boy on the Rocks, such utterly charming scenes as The Football Players and Père Juniet's Cart, and the mesmerically beautiful Sleeping Gypsy. The words of another great eccentric artist, William Blake, could well be applied to Rousseau: 'He who does not imagine in stronger and better lineaments and in stronger and better light than his perishing and mortal eye can see, does not imagine at all.'

Surprised! (Tropical Storm with a Tiger) *1891*
50½″ × 62″ National Gallery, London

This was the first of Rousseau's jungle scenes, the type of painting for which he is now best known. It conveys with extraordinary conviction the feverish intensity of a tropical storm, the slanting lines of the rain, the stripes of the terrified tiger and the lightning in the sky filling the picture with dynamic diagonal movement. At one time it was thought that Rousseau had been to Mexico in his youth and seen tropical flora and fauna there, but this story is now discounted; the inspiration for his jungle scenes came rather from illustrated books and from visits to the zoo and botanical gardens in Paris. In this instance, the tiger was taken from an illustration of a drawing by Delacroix, which Rousseau enlarged with a technical copying instrument known as a pantograph.

Réunion des Musées Nationaux

Portrait of a Woman *1895*
59″ × 39½″ Musée d'Orsay, Paris

*Rousseau's work was generally so little appreciated in his lifetime that
Picasso was able to buy this painting in a junk shop in 1908 for just
a few francs – the shopkeeper thought he might be able to re-use the
canvas. The woman may be a portrait of the artist's second wife,
Joséphine.*

Boy on the Rocks *1895-97*
21¾″ × 18″ National Gallery of Art, Washington

*This startlingly unusual painting is said to have been commissioned
from Rousseau as a memorial to a dead child. Certainly, in spite of its
awkwardness, it has a feeling of gravity appropriate to such a
purpose. Like most of Rousseau's portraits it is presented directly
frontally and has an almost comic-strip clarity and immediacy.*

The Sleeping Gypsy *1897*
51″ × 79″ Collection, The Museum
of Modern Art, New York

*This is one of Rousseau's most unusual
paintings, its enigmatic qualities making
it open to a variety of interpretations.
Just as the Surrealists hailed Rousseau
as one of their predecessors, because of
the painting's strange juxtaposition of
human, animal, still-life and landscape,
so followers of Freud have seen sexual
connotations in the painting. But
however elusive the painting's meaning,
there can be no doubting its eerie and
entrancing beauty; the writer, Jean
Cocteau, called it 'painted poetry'.*

oil on canvas/Gift of Mrs Simon Guggenheim

The Louise and Walter Arensberg Collection

The Merry Jesters *1906*
57½″ × 45″ Philadelphia Museum of Art

The Merry Jesters of the title are the monkeys which are playing with an upturned milk bottle and a back scratcher that have inexplicably appeared in the jungle. It is typical of Rousseau that although the action of the painting is bizarre and elusive in its significance, the picture has a ludicrous logic of its own.

Réunion des Musées Nationaux

The Snake Charmer *1907*
66½" × 74½" Musée d'Orsay, Paris

*This painting was commissioned from Rousseau by the mother of
Robert Delaunay, a painter who admired his work. Madame
Delaunay had been to India, so an exotic subject was appropriate to
her. There are numerous precedents in French painting for pictures of
snake charmers, but Rousseau's darkly sinister figure is totally novel.*

Photo: Carmelo Guadagno

The Football Players *1908*
39½″ × 31½″ Solomon R. Guggenheim Museum, New York

*This is anything but a conventional football match. The men look
more like ballet dancers than sportsmen and the 'pitch' is a small
clearing in an autumnal wood. But in spite of the carefully balanced
composition and the stiffness of the figures, the picture has a buoyant
quality that conveys the physical exhilaration of sport.*

Père Juniet's Cart *1908*
38½″ × 50¾″ Musée de l'Orangerie, Paris

*Monsieur Juniet was a local greengrocer who was particularly proud
of his dappled horse. Rousseau painted this enchanting picture of him
and his family, in which the dogs are as delightfully depicted as the
horse, in settlement of a bill. Rousseau worked from a photograph,
and the man with a hat is believed to be a self-portrait.*

The Dream *1910*
6' 8½" × 9' 9½" Collection,
The Museum
of Modern Art, New York

This huge painting was Rousseau's last work and forms a marvellous conclusion to his career. When he was attacked by a critic for the 'absurdity' of showing a naked woman on a couch in a jungle, the artist replied 'The woman asleep on the couch is dreaming that she has been transported to this forest and that she can hear the enchanter's music. That is the explanation of the couch in the picture'. When the picture was first exhibited Rousseau added the following verses as a subtitle:
'Yadwigha, peacefully asleep, enjoys a lovely dream; she hears a kind snake charmer playing upon his reed. On stream and foliage glisten the silvery beams of the moon and savage serpents listen to the gay, entrancing tune.'
Yadwigha is said to have been a Polish lady with whom Rousseau had been in love.

Animals in Art

Since prehistoric times, Man has expressed fascination for the animal world in paint – creating a kaleidoscope of images which stand as an enduring theme in the history of art.

Animals have always been painted and drawn, but the way in which they are represented in art, and what they mean to Man, has changed enormously through the centuries. At various times they have been seen as sacred creatures to be worshipped; as fierce beasts that threaten human existence; as symbols of the passions and emotions; as exotic representatives of alien cultures; or simply as lovable pets. The manner in which animals are painted, and the qualities that are emphasized, always correspond to the dominant pre-occupations of the age, telling us as much about the changing values of each historical period as it does about animals themselves.

The earliest depictions of animals that survive come from the prehistoric period, and can be seen

Power and awe
(right) These paintings of bison in caves at Lascaux in southern France are the earliest records of human fascination with the animal world. Whether they were painted simply out of admiration, or to give magical power over animals, is a question which has long dogged archaeologists.

Colourphoto Hinz, Allschwil-Basel

in cave paintings like those at Lascaux in south-western France. These depictions of galloping beasts, set beside insignificant, stick-like humans, are records of a time when animals were a constant and highly important feature of everyday life. The graceful lines that describe bison, deer and horses in motion, show how closely the cave painters were able to observe their movements and habits. No one will ever know exactly why people first felt compelled to paint animal images, but the pictures themselves clearly convey the qualities of strength and speed that must have aroused their admiration. This admiration for animals — which seemed in many respects so much more powerful than human beings – even led some prehistoric societies to adopt a particular beast as the symbol of their tribe, and these symbols rapidly became totems to be worshipped and praised.

It was the ancient Egyptians – who appear to have had a genuine love of animals – who first turned totemism into religion, and they carried the veneration of animals to new and sophisticated

Louvre, Paris/Réunion des Musées Nationaux

From pet to goddess
(left) The ancient Egyptians not only worshipped animals as religious deities, they also had a genuine affection for them. The cat was treated as a domestic pet for a thousand years before it became a goddess of pleasure and music.

Bridgeman Art Library

heights. They were the first people to record in painting and sculpture the notion of animals as sacred beings who could give protection to mankind. Nearly all Egyptian deities were given animal aspects. The god Horus, for example, is sometimes shown as a falcon, while Anubis is represented as a wolf, and the goddess Hathor as a cow. Very often these gods were shown as half-beast, half-human, with animal heads and human bodies. This was a combination that the Greeks were to reverse when they invented the mythical centaurs and the harpies, whose lower bodies are animal and whose torsos and heads are human – an apparently more logical arrangement. The Greeks also continued the Egyptian idea of deities being able to turn into animals at will. At the very heart of Greek mythology there is the story of Zeus, who metamorphosed into a bull in order to carry off the unwilling Europa, an episode that was to become a standard subject in Western painting.

THE GENTLE LAMB

The introduction of Christianity to the West brought about a profound change in the way in which men thought about animals and represented them in art. Whereas the favourite symbols of aggressive cultures like Mesopotamia had been the powerful bull and horse, and the ferocious lion, Christianity brought a new awareness of the gentler creatures of the animal kingdom. The meek lamb following its shepherd became a metaphor for the human soul as part of the flock of Christ, who was Himself eventually

Accurate detail
(below) When this was painted in the 1860s, few people would have seen the sharp-billed Toucan – one of the most colourful birds of South America. This, of course, was a good reason to represent it with such accuracy of detail, although the artist was certainly aware of the Toucan's obvious aesthetic appeal.

Creature of myth
(left) Part goat, part horse, the mythical unicorn was revered in the Middle Ages for its magical properties. The unicorn's horn was believed to be an antidote to poison and it could be captured only by a virgin, in whose lap it would lay its head. This picture is taken from a series of tapestries entitled the Lady and the Unicorn, *which was discovered in 1844, the year of Rousseau's birth, in a château in Creuse, France. Displayed at the Cluny museum forty years later, these tapestries may well have influenced Rousseau's art in their elaborate detail.*

Musée Cluny, Paris

A popular Victorian animal artist
(left) More than any other British artist, Sir Edwin Landseer is renowned for his talent for sentimentalizing animals. It is this that made him the most popular painter of his day. To emphasize this painting's emotional appeal, Landseer changed its title from Dogs, *to the more grandiose* Dignity and Impudence.

referred to as 'the Lamb of God'. The peaceful dove became an emblem of the Holy Spirit, replacing the majestic hawks and eagles favoured by earlier civilizations. The old animal symbols did, however, survive in the emblems chosen to represent the Evangelists: the lion for St Mark, the eagle for St John, the ox for St Luke, and, as if to reinforce Man's link with the natural world, the human being for St Matthew.

MEDIEVAL MYTHS

For centuries, the Evangelist symbols were almost the only animals represented in Western art. But during the Middle Ages, curiosity about other creatures – real and imaginary – led to new developments. The writhing monsters that twine themselves around the columns and arches of Romanesque churches expressed a new sense of the power of evil, and human fear of eternal damnation. Yet the medieval bestiaries – manuscripts devoted to legends and folklore about animals – portray beasts as the holders of a divine wisdom which is revealed in their actions. The most enchanting of all medieval animals is, however, the imaginary unicorn – part horse, part goat, with a horn imbued with magical properties – which found its way into manuscripts and tapestries during the 14th century. Legend had it that this strange beast could only be captured by a virgin, in whose lap it would lay its head in submission. This connection with virginity gave it a convenient link with Christianity, through the Virgin Mary, just as its ability to purify whatever it touched with its horn related it to Christ.

The unicorn vanished from art during the Renaissance period, when artists began to feel that it was more important to portray the real world than a make-believe one. While medieval artists depicted animals in a rather stylized manner,

Renaissance painters started to look at them more carefully, and even to sketch animals from the life. Dürer, who kept many pets himself, is a good example of an artist who observed both exotic animals – like walruses and whales – and familiar ones like the hare.

It soon became apparent that, unlike some people, animals do not have to be flattered in art, and animal painting offered great scope for artists who wished to portray natural appearances as truthfully as possible. This spirit of scientific enquiry was at its height during the 18th century, and especially evident in Thomas Bewick's delicate woodcuts of birds and animals.

During Bewick's lifetime, however, there was a subtle shift towards a more subjective attitude about animals. Bewick's great contemporary, George Stubbs, saw no necessary contradiction between an obsession with anatomical accuracy in the horses he depicted, and the highly contrived pictures he painted of them locked in combat with lions. Artists of the Romantic period began, similarly, to celebrate the animal ferocity they had

previously abhorred. As the great Romantic poet and artist, William Blake, once wrote: 'The Tigers of Wrath are wiser than the Horses of Instruction.' Delacroix also exulted in the intensity of animal combat which reflected his own deeply held conviction that, 'men are tigers and wolves bent on destroying one another'.

VICTORIAN PRIDE

These visions of violence were symptomatic of a troubled age, and did not survive in the more secure worlds of Victorian Britain or Second Empire France. The Victorians and their European contemporaries much preferred paintings of animals in which they could see some gentler human feeling, and they particularly enjoyed the sight of domestic pets displaying all the human emotions of sadness, pride, solemnity, impudence and, above all, loyalty to their masters. It is small wonder that Sir Edwin Landseer – the artist who invested animals with human characteristics – became the most popular painter of his day.

Visual Arts Library

Rosseau/Tropical Landscape/Norton Simon Museum, Los Angeles

The lion's wrath
(left) Although George Stubbs is most famous for his detailed paintings of racing horses, he was also fascinated by wild and exotic animals like zebras, cheetahs and leopards, which were being imported into Britain. In this painting of 1770, it is the ferocity of the animals that captured Stubbs' imagination, and also later inspired the French Romantics.

Tropical Monkeys
(above) Before painting his luminous and colourful Exotic Landscape, Rousseau studied photographs of the leaf monkey, which he went on to recreate with meticulous detail. But in making the monkeys' postures and faces, and playful antics almost human, he transforms the animal world, bringing it strangely closer to our own.

The changing ideals of the 20th century meant that artists could no longer see animals as representative of any definable human virtues. In the exotic landscapes of Rousseau, for example, lions and apes take on a frozen, static quality which belies the artist's scrupulous attention to detail; in the paintings of the German Expressionist Franz Marc, cows and horses are painted in rich reds and blues – colours that are expressive of their innate qualities. Marc emphasized the difference of his own, highly individual approach, when he wrote: 'How wretched, how soulless, is our habit of placing animals in a landscape which mirrors our own vision, instead of sinking ourselves in the soul of the animal so as to imagine its perceptions.'

A modern vision
(left) It was the innocence and physical grace of animals which led Franz Marc to develop his highly personal style of painting. Searching for ways to express his pantheistic belief in the spirituality of animals, he evolved a symbolic use of form and colour which made him reject his naturalistic beginnings. His striking red and blue horses are an attempt to portray the essential gentleness and mystery of animals, without focusing solely on their physical appearance.

Joachim Blauel – Artothek

Franz Marc/Red and Blue Horses/Stadt. Galerie im Lenbachhaus, Munich

A Year in the Life 1910

In the last year of Rousseau's life, France was paralysed by industrial conflict, there was a constitutional crisis in Britain, and the Portuguese monarchy was overthrown. While English critics were still being shocked by the 'crudities' of Post-Impressionism, the new Italian movement, Futurism, was already in its second year.

For several years France had suffered from industrial unrest, with vineyard workers striking for better conditions and civil servants demanding the right to unionize. When French railway workers went on strike in 1910, Aristide Briand, despite having been a socialist himself, called out the army, using the argument that the railways were 'essential to the life of the nation'. Briand's appeal to force was successful, since he was able to conscript those railwaymen who were army reservists and order them back to work at their old jobs. Disobedience now meant not dismissal, but execution as a mutineer. Inevitably, the strike collapsed.

The political crisis in Britain was to last for over two years. In 1909, the Conservative-dominated House of Lords rejected the Liberal's Finance Act incorporating Lloyd George's radical

Stravinsky's Firebird
(below and right) Diaghilev's repertoire for his second Paris season (1910) with the Ballets Russes included a new ballet, The Firebird, *with music by a little known Russian composer, the 28 year old Igor Stravinsky. The title role of the magical bird (right) who helps Prince Ivan rescue a beautiful princess and her companions from the spell of an evil magician was danced by Karsavina. This, Stravinsky's first ballet score, was an immediate success and was followed shortly by two more –* Petrushka *and* The Rite of Spring.

Novosti

Ilya Repin/Tolstoy Ploughing/Tretyakov State Gallery, Moscow

Tolstoy the peasant
(above) Towards the end of his life, the world famous novelist Lev Nikolaevich Tolstoy evolved his own form of metaphysic (Tolstoyism) and adopted a peasant mode of life. This led over the years to tremendous family tensions which ultimately caused the author of War and Peace *and* Anna Karenina *to secretly leave his beloved ancestral country estate Yasnaya Polyana on 28 October 1910, accompanied by his daughter. The 82 year old Tolstoy, who was wandering aimlessly, collapsed soon after at Astapovo railway station and died on 7 November.*

'Peer versus the people'
(right) Lloyd George's Liberal 'People's Budget' of 1909 was designed to raise revenue particularly for the Navy and old age pensions. A graduated tax was proposed for large incomes and a revenue tax on land. The latter, predictably perhaps, was considered as a direct attack by the predominantly landowning House of Lords who rejected the budget, contrary to constitutional custom, forcing a general election for 1910. This Conservative election poster shows the Liberal 'thief' stealing unearned income from ground rent, watched by a tenant fearful for her shares.

Lords Gallery, London

ELECTORS SUPPORT AN HONEST POLICY NOT ROBBERY

BY VOTING FOR THE UNIONIST CANDIDATE

E.T. Archive

Musée d'Orsay, Paris

40

'People's Budget', which aimed to levy taxes on the rich that were, by contemporary standards, unusually heavy. Since the Lords' action broke the tacit constitutional agreement that Bills dealing with finance would not be obstructed, Asquith's Liberal government determined to abolish the Lords' absolute veto on legislation. The death of Edward VII and accession of George V complicated matters, necessitating general elections in January and again in December 1910. The Lords, knowing that the King would, if necessary, create hundreds of new peers to bring about a Liberal majority, were eventually obliged to pass the Act of Parliament that restricted their powers in August 1911.

Portugal had been financially and politically unstable for some years before the revolution of 1910. The King and the heir to the throne had been assassinated in 1908, and under the inexperienced Manuel II, the old political parties engaged in futile intrigues while the rebel Republican cause gained strength in the capital, Lisbon, and in the navy. To head off growing agitation against the power of the church, Manuel ordered the suppression of Jesuit houses on 3 October, but he was too late. The following day, two warships began to bombard the royal palace. The rebel sailors landed and advanced into Lisbon with the result that the unfortunate Manuel fled to England and Portugal was declared a republic.

In spite of these domestic upheavals, the world seemed a safer place as international tension relaxed. Russian fears of Austrian expansion in the Balkans were quieted by an agreement between the two powers to maintain the *status quo* in the area. Russia and Germany were also reconciled. Tsar

Bibliothèque l'Arsenale, Paris

Giancarlo Costa

George V and Queen Mary

(above) On 6 May 1910, Edward VII, whose nine year reign had given his name to an era, died aged 69. He left behind a constitutional deadlock created by the House of Lords' refusal to pass the 1909 Liberal Budget. As a result, the government had been forced to call a general election in January 1910, but they needed Irish support to gain a clear majority in parliament and pass the budget. This was only forthcoming if the Liberals agreed to support an Irish Home Rule Bill and prevented the Lords from once again exercising their veto. The new king, George V, was obliged to secretly assure the Liberals that if they won the December election he would create as many Liberal peers as were necessary to pass the Parliament Bill that would muzzle the Lords. The Upper House was forced to concede defeat in 1911.

Nicholas II visited Kaiser Wilhelm II at Potsdam and ended their disputes over the Middle East by an agreement whereby the Russians were given a free hand in northern Persia if they undertook not to oppose Germany's Baghdad Railway.

FUTURISM IN ITS SECOND YEAR

In February 1910, Umberto Boccioni and four other Italian artists published the Manifesto of Futurist Painters, which denounced attachment to the past and glorified action, speed and the dynamism of the machine. Nine months later the critic and painter Roger Fry mounted the first Post-Impressionist exhibition in London. The 150 paintings by Manet, Cézanne, Gauguin, Van Gogh and the Fauves were disliked by the large majority of spectators brought up on the conventions of Victorian academic art.

In 1910, Florence Nightingale, the intrepid lady who had revolutionized nursing during the Crimean War of 1854-6, died. So did the writers Leo Tolstoy and Mark Twain, while Dr. Crippen was hanged for murdering his wife. The Turks suppressed a revolt in Albania with much bloodshed and struggled to maintain their hold on Arabia, where they were challenged by the militant Wahabi sect led by Ibn Saud. The Viceroy of British India was injured by an anarchist bomb; the premier of British-dominated Egypt was assassinated by nationalists. In the newly formed Union of South Africa, rival political parties were founded, and in September Louis Botha's South African Party defeated the Unionists.

A life for a life
(right) Hawley Harvey Crippen was an American by birth who had emigrated to London in 1900. His music-hall star wife had long treated the little doctor with unconcealed boredom and contempt, with the inevitable result that he sought solace outside the bounds of matrimony. The lady concerned was Ethel le Neve, a young typist working for one of the minor medical firms with which Crippen was associated. In mid-January 1910 the Doctor ordered five grains of a poisonous compound; Cora Crippen was seen alive for the last time on 31 January. Her disappearance was explained away as a business visit to America and her subsequent demise there. Meanwhile Crippen was foolishly dressing le Neve in his wife's jewellery and later taking her into his home. Police suspicions were aroused and a routine call ascertained that both had fled. A search of the house made the grisly discovery of dismembered portions of a headless body, wrapped in a pyjama jacket, which was soon identified as belonging to Mrs Crippen. Meanwhile the murderer and his young lover were on an ocean liner bound for Quebec, posing as father and son. The captain's suspicions were alerted by certain anomalies and for the first time wireless was used to notify the police. They crossed over to Quebec on a faster boat to arrest 'Mr and Master Robinson'. Crippen maintained his innocence throughout the subsequent trial but the evidence was incontrovertible. Ethel le Neve was acquitted but Crippen ended his days in a hangman's noose at Pentonville Prison on 23 November 1910.

PAUL KLEE

1879-1940

Paul Klee is recognized as one of the great figures of 20th century art, a painter whose interest in naive and oriental work allowed him to develop a childlike innocence of vision that transformed the familiar world into one of 'music and poetry'. Klee was also one of the finest teachers of this century. A serious-minded man, he adapted his theories for a teaching programme at the Bauhaus which has been widely followed since.

Klee knew many of the leading artists of his generation, but while most of his contemporaries clung to specific groups and styles, Klee's career was both highly individual and totally single-minded. Dismissed from his post at Dusseldorf by the Nazis, Klee saw out his last years in Switzerland where, despite a long and painful illness, he continued to work, constantly extending the boundaries of his art.

An Imaginative Introvert

Klee was born in Switzerland and came of a musical family. He wrote poetry, but chose art as a career. Much of his inspiration came from his travels to North Africa.

Felix Klee/COSMOPRESS, Geneva

typical of much established art of the period. There was, however, a livelier side to the Bavarian capital represented by the Secessionists and their magazine *Die Jugend* which gave its name to 'Jugendstil' – the German version of Art Nouveau. Another magazine, *Simplicissimus*, with its biting satirical cartoons also appealed to the young artist.

On his return to Berne in 1901, this combination of symbolism and satire formed the basis for Klee's first mature works; a series of etchings or 'inventions'. These bizarre figures and animals have a strong sense of irony, but there is an unusually bitter streak in their harsh lines and physical distortions. By 1906, when he married the

Paul and his sister
(left) Mathilde, Paul's sister, was three when he was born, and later became her brother's model. Paul showed an early talent for drawing which was encouraged by his maternal grandmother, who gave him his first box of chalks at four.

Childhood in Berne
(below) Klee's family home was a small house with a garden on the outskirts of Berne. Through visits to relatives, Klee knew the surrounding countryside. After studying in Munich, he returned home until his marriage in 1906.

Key Dates

1879 born near Berne, Switzerland

1898 moves to Munich to study art

1901 visits Italy

1906 marries pianist Lily Stumpf

1907 birth of Felix

1911 meets *Blaue Reiter* group

1914 visits Tunisia

1916 death of Marc; joins army

1920 begins teaching at Bauhaus

1928-9 visits Egypt

1933 dismissed from post by Nazis; moves back to Berne

1940 dies at Muralto-Locarno

Paul Klee was born on 18 December 1879, at Munchenbuchsee, near Berne in Switzerland. His father, a Bavarian, was an organist and music teacher in a nearby college while his mother, who came from Basle, was an adept pianist. Klee's childhood was therefore dominated by music. With his mother's encouragement, he became an accomplished violinist and throughout his life music, particularly that of Mozart, was to be a constant source of delight and inspiration.

In his youth Klee showed some ability as a poet, but by the time he had finished his school education it was clear where his main interests lay. The brief autobiography written at the end of his life records this conclusion to his childhood: 'I had ample choice of profession. My school leaving-certificate meant that I could have taken up anything, but I wanted to become a painter and to devote my life to art. At that time – and even today – this meant going abroad. The only choice I had to make lay between Paris and Germany. My own feelings in the matter took me to Germany.'

In 1898, Klee moved to Munich to study painting, at first in the school of Edwin Knirr and later in the Academy under the imperious Franz von Stuck, whose rather gloomy classicism was

Image Bank/Tom Tracy

ways Klee was preparing himself for the use of colour. As early as 1901, on a trip to Italy, he had been greatly impressed by the colour and vivacity of Mediterranean life and over the next decade the work of Cézanne, Matisse and particularly Van Gogh (whose work he saw on exhibition in 1908), all great colourists, had a marked effect on him.

TOWARDS COLOUR

In 1911, Klee's move to colour was given further encouragement when he first came into close contact with the *Blaue Reiter* group. This circle, including Kandinsky, Franz Marc, Alfred Kubin, Alexei von Jawlensky and Auguste Macke, was committed to a more expressive handling of colour, partly inspired by music, but equally placing great emphasis on mysticism and primitive art. Klee, who felt a strong affinity with their work and ideas, felt encouraged to pursue his own interest in children's art and in 1912 he exhibited several works in the second *Blaue Reiter* exhibition

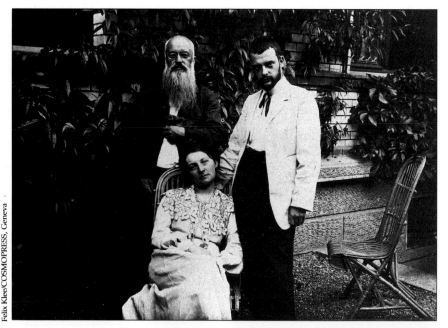

A musical family
Paul Klee's father, shown with Klee and Lily Stumpf after their marriage, was a music teacher and his mother took him to concerts and opera, where he particularly enjoyed the works of Mozart (right). Lily, a pianist, kept their family during the first 15 years of marriage by teaching music.

Scene from Mozart's *Magic Flute*

pianist Lily Stumpf, Klee felt ready to exhibit these works and the couple moved to Munich, but there was very little interest in his pictures.

Throughout this period, Klee was deliberately restricting himself to the materials and techniques of the graphic arts; black and white prints and drawings with great emphasis on a crisp linear style. This reflected his interest in the work of such artists as Goya, Redon, Blake and James Ensor, who had likewise explored a world of fantasy and imagination. It is clear, however, that in various

of prints and drawings. That same year he developed an interest in the French painter Robert Delaunay and his theories of light and colour, although the bulk of his work was still largely executed in black and white. It was not for a further two years that a turning point was reached.

On 5 April 1914, Klee and two companions, the painters Louis Moilliet and Auguste Macke, set out for Tunisia visiting Tunis, Hammamet and Kairouan, where the shock of the light and colour immediately stirred Klee's imagination. At

Kairouan – the ancient city of a hundred mosques – he encountered a combination of fantasy, mirage and ancient fairy tale, for the spectacle of domes, palm trees, minarets and colourful costumes was overwhelming. After only two weeks Klee left in no doubt that his life, as well as his art, had been transformed. 'Colour possesses me' he wrote. 'I no longer need to pursue it; it possesses me for ever, I know. That is the revelation of this blessed moment. Colour and I are one. I am a painter.'

In the months that followed, Klee was engaged in such intense activity inspired by these experiences that the outbreak of the First World War did not seem to interrupt his work. However, such seclusion could not last for long. His circle of friends was soon dispersed to different parts of Europe and the hostilities quickly began to have their effect. Within days of arriving at the Front, Macke was killed and two years later, the death of Franz Marc at Verdun plunged Klee into a trough of despair and introspection that affected him for the rest of his life. Marc, Klee's closest friend, had always seemed the more human and vital of the two and the news of his death evoked terrible images of destruction and collapse in his mind. A week later Klee, who had German citizenship, was called up to join the army.

As a man of 37, Klee's military duties were fairly light and he was able to continue working on drawings and watercolours while in uniform. By the time of his release at the end of the war, his years of patient study were ready to bear fruit. Now the master of his art and able to translate the imagery of his inner world into paintings, Klee was also beginning to receive popular and critical acclaim for his exhibitions. Then, on 25 November 1920, his career took another important turn when he received a telegram inviting him to join the Bauhaus as a painter.

The Bauhaus had been set up as an experimental college in the belief that teachers experienced in different fields could collaborate in

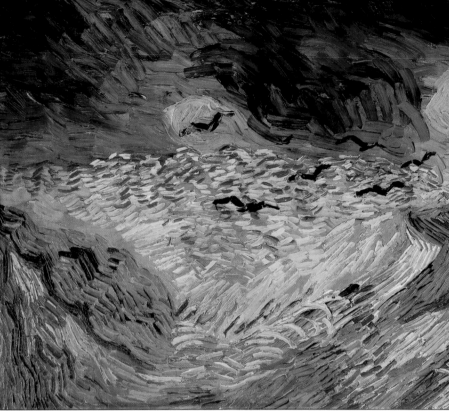

Stedelijk Museum, Amsterdam

the training of a new generation of architects and designers. Under Walter Gropius, the first director and guiding spirit, the visual arts were regarded as an essential component in the education programme alongside various craft skills. Accordingly, Klee had his own studio and participated in many of the college activities. For perhaps the first time, he and his family enjoyed financial security, but more than this he welcomed the sense of community shared with fellow artists, notably Kandinsky who joined the staff the following year.

Influence of Van Gogh
(above) In 1908, Klee saw two exhibitions of Van Gogh which had a huge impact: 'Here one sees a mind consumed by cosmic conflagration. On the eve of the catastrophe, he liberates himself through work.' But Van Gogh's paroxysms also disturbed the orderly Klee.

Tunisia
(left) The first high point in Klee's artistic development took place on his trip to Tunisia in April 1914. Until then, he had concentrated on graphic art, but the power and translucency of the African sunlight came as a revelation to him: 'The sun has a dark force. The colourful clarity of the landscape is full of promise.' Absorbing the effect of light around him, Klee at last felt he understood colour and rushed back home after two weeks, eager to start painting.

Image Bank/Gerard Champlong

At this time the Bauhaus was most remarkable for the freedom and innovation of its teaching in which the students were encouraged to adopt a more imaginative and open-minded approach to design problems. Klee's contribution was to develop a series of technical exercises examining the basic qualities of lines, planes and textures: in essence, the raw materials of pictorial art which could be explored like a formal vocabulary. These studies he later described in several texts, notably the *Pedagogical Sketchbook* of 1925, which has since become a manual for the teaching of art in both Europe and America.

A GROWING REPUTATION

While he was working at the Bauhaus, Klee's reputation as a painter continued to rise and exhibitions of his work were held throughout Germany and abroad. A case in point was the famous Exhibition of Surrealist Art held in Paris in 1925 where he was hailed by André Breton as an ally of their movement. He was also able to indulge his love for travel and scarcely a year went past when he did not visit either Italy or France.

In December 1928, Klee set out on his most ambitious journey, to Egypt. Klee had been interested in Egyptian art since his earliest visits to museums, but it was not until he saw the monumental remains of Luxor and Karnak that he found a deeper understanding of the ancient civilization and a unity between the present and the past. As with the previous trip to Tunisia, this experience was like a mixture of fantasy and reality

The Artistic Centre of Munich

Munich was a lively, cosmopolitan centre with a long tradition in the visual arts. When Klee arrived there in the 1890s, he stayed in Schwabing, the bohemian quarter. At the time, the city had a strong 'Secessionist' group opposed to the traditional academy, and over the next three decades Munich became host to a succession of avant-garde movements. Klee's closest links were with the Expressionist painters Kandinsky, Macke, Jawlensky and Marc, who took the name *Blaue Reiter* from the magazine they published in 1911. But he also knew such figures as Hugo Ball and Hans Arp who were founders of the Dada group and the Cabaret Voltaire in Zurich during World War I.

Hugo Ball
(right) *The Dada poet, Hugo Ball, was a great admirer of Klee's work and pursued a similar line to Klee, namely to create 'a sublime wisdom palpable not in unrestrained outbursts of feeling, but under a mask simultaneously absurd and tragic'. Here he is reciting his 'poem without words' in a Cubist costume.*

Franz Marc
(below) *Marc's* Fighting Forms *shows his maturity as an artist, unlike Klee who at the time was limited to graphic art. But they shared the aim of finding a new means of expression and were also good friends. Klee was devastated by Marc's death.*

Archiv für Kunst und Geschichte

Staatsgalerie moderner Kunst, München

Blauel-Gnamm/Artothek

The Bauhaus Years
(left) In November 1920, Klee was invited to join the staff of the Bauhaus, the revolutionary new art college set up the previous year by the architect Walter Gropius. His years at the Bauhaus were amongst the happiest of his life – he was given his own studio, and enjoyed the company of his fellow artists, particularly that of his friend Kandinsky. This photograph shows the staff of the Bauhaus in 1926, shortly after its move to Dessau. Klee stands fourth from the right, with Kandinsky on his right.

and for the remainder of his life stylized pyramids and exotic flora would appear in his paintings.

During this time, the increasingly authoritarian bias of German society was becoming hostile to the Bauhaus and outside pressure led first to its transfer from Weimar to Dessau, and eventually to its closure in 1933. By that time, many of the original staff had moved on and, when Klee was invited to teach at the Dusseldorf Academy in 1931, he willingly accepted. The new post seemed ideal since it allowed him to concentrate on painting, but the political climate was rapidly deteriorating. Two years later when the swastika was raised over the school, Klee was forced to resign and by the end of 1933, he had to leave Germany for good.

RETURN TO SWITZERLAND

For the second time in his life, Klee's world was disrupted and his friends scattered over Europe, but on this occasion their art also came under attack. Hounded from their posts, modern artists were alternately banned and ridiculed by the new regime. At the notorious exhibition of Degenerate Art held in Munich in 1937, 17 of Klee's paintings were hung alongside the work of the leading figures in the German avant-garde, firmly outlining the Nazi party's opposition to any progressive tendencies in the arts. In the face of such hostility, Klee returned to Switzerland where the enforced retirement from teaching allowed him to devote more time to his own work.

Settling again in Berne, Klee was by no means isolated. He was able to travel to France and Italy and he received many friends at his home. Furthermore, his return to Switzerland had been

Impressions of Egypt

On 17 December 1928, Klee embarked from Genoa for Egypt, thus fulfilling a long-felt ambition to visit the cradle of the ancient civilizations. His journey took him up the Nile Valley from Cairo to the great temple sites at Luxor, Karnak, Thebes and Assouan. Like his earlier trip to Tunisia, the visit was short, lasting only three weeks, but the experience was decisive. The effect of the light, the open landscape and the ruined monuments to ancient gods and rulers combined to create a powerful impression on the artist's mind. This was the raw material of his late work and the inspiration for some of his finest paintings, such as *Monument in a Fertile Country* (pp.62-3).

Splendour in stone
(right) This statue of Rameses II stands on the temple site of Luxor, one of Klee's ports of call. Klee admired the massive simplicity of ancient Egyptian art.

A magical landscape
(below) Klee was deeply impressed by the wide, open strata of the desert landscape. In his paintings, he recaptured the scenery in stripes of colour.

Nazi censorship
(right) Klee was ignominiously dismissed from the Dusseldorf Academy by the Nazis in 1933. The following year, a book on Klee's drawings was confiscated by the Gestapo. Like many of his avant-garde contemporaries, particularly the German Expressionists, Klee was considered to be dangerous and his art degenerate. Seventeen of his works were included in an exhibition of Degenerate Art set up by Hitler in 1937 to illustrate the progressive tendencies he sought to eliminate. Here, Hitler surveys his assembly of despised art.

marked by a major retrospective exhibition in 1935, making him something of a celebrity in his native country. This should have been the preamble to a more settled, mature phase when Klee's achievement would be finally confirmed, but that same year saw the first signs of the illness that overshadowed his last years and finally killed him.

Initially diagnosed as bronchitis, Klee was later found to be suffering from a rare and progressively debilitating disease now known as scleroderma. The progress of the disease is irreversible and eventually attacks the whole body. Despite the discomfort and the obvious restrictions that the illness placed on his work, Klee was still capable of bursts of intense activity. It was the character of his work, however, that changed towards a distinct darkening of the spirit brought on by his awareness of death. Titles of late works such as *Death and Fire* (p.67) are suggestive of his frame of mind. Occasional visitors served to lighten the burden of these last years and in 1937, Picasso, Braque and Kirchner visited the artist giving him a sense of contact with the outside world.

At times, the course of events in Europe must have seemed like a grotesque parody of his own condition. Klee had already written that he could not live through another war and he was spared that experience. On 10 May 1940, the day Hitler's army invaded western Europe, Klee entered the nursing home at Locarno-Orselina. His condition deteriorated and he was moved to the clinic at Muralto where he died on 29 June. On his gravestone at Schlosshalden there is a short passage from his journal: 'In this world I cannot be wholly understood. So I am better among the dead, or among the unborn. Closer than most to the centre of creation, but still not close enough.'

The Innocent Eye

Klee's works abound with radiant colour harmonies and simple shapes drawn from the natural world. Because of their apparent simplicity, his paintings have often been likened to child art.

Taken as a whole, Klee's work presents the spectator with certain problems because his large output, close to 10,000 works, has no real unity of style. Rather than adopting a specific technique, Klee was more concerned with allowing the work to assume its own natural form. He described the artist as an instrument through which larger, more elemental forces were channelled, the artist's function being to organize this complex material and to present it in a way that makes sense to others. For this reason, Klee has often been linked to both the Expressionists and the Surrealists, but he was very much his own man, following paths that were of his own making.

The essence of Klee's work lies in his belief in a spirit or life-force that operates through all things. His job, therefore, was not to copy nature but to recognize the process at work and, as in nature, to allow the work of art to grow. Klee described his views in a well-known lecture using the analogy of

Hans Hinz/© ADAGP, Paris/COSMOPRESS, Geneva, 1988

181 'BALDGREIS' (Senecio) 1922/40.5cm × 38cm/Gemälde, Ölfarben, Karton, Schirting aufgeklebt, kreidegrundartig signiert links unten

The Virgin in the Tree
(below) In his early career, Klee concentrated on etching, a medium which allowed him to explore the expressive qualities of line. In this etching, angular lines of the woman and the tree create an image of barrenness and desiccation.

Senecio (1922)
(right) In this enigmatic head, Klee captures the expressive simplicity of a child's drawing. Using basic geometric shapes, he creates a face which quivers with life, the 'eyebrows' and 'mouth' producing a wry and whimsical expression.

Kunstmuseum, Basel

Paul Klee Foundation, Kunst Museum, Bern/© ADAGP, Paris/COSMOPRESS, Geneva, 1988

1903, 'JUNGFRAU IM BAUM – TRAUMEND' Radierung auf Zink/23,6×29,8/Invention 2/Kornfeld No. 6

a tree. As the roots transmit the sap to the trunk from which the crown of the tree unfolds, so the artist moulds his experience into his work. Nobody would expect the crown of the tree to be a mirror-image of the roots, so the final work of art is not merely an imitation of its model.

Klee insisted on the need to 'enter into the secret of the creative drive to form; to trace the path to creation'. His aim was to penetrate to the heart of this simple but profound mystery. For Klee, the finished painting should convey some sense of the pattern of thought behind it – of the ideas and associations which gradually give rise to the final artistic image.

As a result Klee spent most of his life developing that simplicity of vision that he so admired in the child's response to the world. In Klee's view, children's drawings were superior to his own because they had not been 'trickled through the brain'. He was similarly indifferent to

Collection, The Museum of Modern Art, New York 13⅛" × 13⅛"/oil on cardboard

Fire in the Evening
(above) Klee discovered the full potential of colour after his visit to Tunisia. Here, an ordered pattern of brightly coloured stripes evokes in an abstract way the visual experience of a fire at dusk. The orange shape in the centre locates the fire itself.

Still Life (1940)
(right) This was Klee's last work and remained unfinished at his death. Klee mixes here natural and manmade objects in a way which emphasises their formal and spiritual affinity as, for example, the table top echoes the shape of the full moon.

historical and cultural barriers. An Egyptian sculpture spoke as profoundly about the true nature of the world as a work by Michelangelo or Rembrandt, and Klee felt confident in selecting elements from various sources even in the development of a single picture.

SPACE AND COLOUR

While there is no distinct style of Klee's work, there are one or two features of his art that do bear analysis since, despite his unique interpretation, they are derived from other artists. The first of these is his debt to the Cubists. As an overall pictorial method, Cubism had very little to offer Klee. Picasso and Braque were concerned with objects in the physical world that Klee, with his interest in growth, can have found little sympathy with. Nevertheless, they had developed a way of painting in which solid three-dimensional motifs

seen from different viewpoints could be reconstructed on the flat canvas in a composition of lines and planes. A brief glimpse at such works as *Full Moon* (p.58) or *Monument in a Fertile Country* (pp.62-3), should be enough for us to recognize the way in which Klee similarly organizes his pictures with a crisp linear design that nevertheless creates a sense of space.

The other feature of Klee's work that links him to his contemporaries is his use of colour. It is significant that of all the painters in the Cubist circle, Klee should find the greatest affinity with Robert Delaunay. The French artist had attempted to introduce the effect of light into his 'window paintings' with the light broken up into delicate colour squares as if seen through a prism. Klee was fascinated by this and translated Delaunay's most important theoretical essay into German.

At the same time, around 1912, Klee was also interested in the way colour could be used as an independent element in painting, free from the need to describe things. Like his friends in the *Blaue Reiter* group, notably Kandinsky and Marc, he felt that colour was similar to music and that a picture could, in a sense, be orchestrated. He wrote in his diary, 'I shall have to be capable of improvizing freely on the colour keyboard of my watercolour pots'. When the full potential of colour was revealed to him during his trip to Tunisia, he was able to translate his visions into paintings and even in the 1920s, when his art

assumed a genuinely independent character, these features remained an essential part. Even when used to describe recognizable forms, Klee's colours can be read as a series of visual 'chords'.

A WORLD OF FANTASY

By the 1920s, Klee had long since left behind the techniques of different schools and had come to rely on the primacy of his own vision. This he explored by allowing simple irrational studies to develop their own logic. There are hundreds of sheets covered with drawings rather like doodles, in which various shapes have been worked up into humorous, absurd and occasionally sinister images. This world of fantasy was nevertheless a disciplined and orderly creation. It has an organic life of its own, not necessarily similar, but parallel to the world of 'reality'. In paintings such as *Fish Magic* (pp.60-61), we can observe Klee creating an order in the relationship of the abstract shapes as well as of the natural objects, and this order operates throughout the picture.

In his last years, much of the playfulness and delight in creating new worlds disappeared from Klee's art. In the face of his physical decline he chose to present images of much greater starkness and power. He also began to work on a larger scale, while maintaining his imaginative use of materials. In this, he had always been experimental, employing various textures, shapes and colours wherever he found them. Ancient inscriptions, woven carpets, leaves, basketwork all reappeared in one form or another. In his late work, however, Klee began to experiment with the paint surface itself. We can find pictures on paper stuck to canvas, sack cloth stained and mounted on board, gesso and plaster painted and inscribed and combinations of canvas, newsprint, chalk, pastel, watercolours and oil paints. At the same time his images became simpler and more economical, and his colours more subdued.

Until the end of his life, indeed until the last days in June 1940, Klee continued to experiment and to pursue his solitary vision. At his death, an unfinished *Still Life* (p.51) remained on his easel.

Archetypes and Symbols

Klee constantly sought to express himself in primal 'uncorrupt' symbols and archetypes. This explains something of his fascination with Oriental art, and particularly with Egyptian mythological sculpture. The actual subject of a statue or the meaning of a hieroglyphic inscription was of less importance to Klee than the underlying sense of a timeless truth. By using such sources in his paintings, he was attempting to give these ancient artefacts a new meaning that preserved their essential quality. Art for Klee was not intended to reproduce the visible, but to reveal something deeper – the reality beyond appearances.

Ardea

Michael Holford

Egyptian hieroglyphs
(left) Like Klee's paintings, hieroglyphs combine familiar images with abstract symbols in seemingly irrational patterns. Many of the symbols shown here, like the bird and the open eye, recur in Klee's works.

The Egyptian God, Thoth
(right) The Egyptian God, Thoth, the God of Learning, was sometimes represented in animal form, but more often, as here, as a man with the head of an ibis. The combination of human and bird forms, and the simple shapes, had great appeal for Klee.

LOOKING AT A MASTERPIECE

Landscape with Yellow Birds

Klee came to colour only gradually. For over ten years he worked mainly in black and white and it was not until his trip to Tunisia in 1914 that the brilliance of the light and the exotic splendour of his surroundings converted him to a richer use of colour. In *Landscape with Yellow Birds*, a watercolour from 1923, the use of contrasted colour is particularly marked. The birds (detail right) seem to stand out from their darker background, creating a curious sense of space. At the same time, the whole picture can be seen as an arrangement of coloured shapes. It may also reflect Klee's interest in the symbolic colour of Oriental art.

TRADEMARKS

Mastery of Colour

Klee was a master of colour which he used not only in a representational way, but as a medium in itself, to evoke a spiritual response. He compared colour to music which can move us without having a subject, and his colours function on this level, as a form of visual harmony.

1923, 32 'LANDSCHAFT MIT GELBEN VOGELN' Aquarell, Zeichenpapier, schwarz grundiert, schwarz grundiert/35,5:44/signiert rechts unten/Privatbesitz Schweiz

Private Collection/Hans Hinz/© ADAGP, Paris/COSMOPRESS Geneva, 1988

Gallery

Klee's work is among the most varied and complex of any 20th century artist. His output was enormous, but he never repeated himself, and he moved with ease from representational art to almost pure abstraction. He was accomplished in oil and watercolour, and sometimes combined the two, as in Fish Magic. Often he was

Motif of Hammamet *1914*
8″ × 6″ Kupferstichkabinett Museum, Basel

Until 1914, Klee worked almost exclusively in black and white, but in that year he visited Tunisia and, like Delacroix before him, was bowled over by the brilliant colours he saw there. Here, specific forms give way to a patchwork of bright colour, recreating Klee's vision of a dazzling Tunisian town.

directly inspired by the events of his life (for example his visits to Tunisia and Egypt, which resulted in paintings such as Motif of Hammamet and Monument in a Fertile Country), but generally it was his own extraordinarily vivid imagination that provided the source for his explorations of the fantasies and fears of mankind.

It is the joyous spirit of Klee's work – the delightful humour of The Twittering Machine or the vibrant splendour of Ad Parnassum – that has made him so deservedly popular, but in his late works, particularly the astonishingly intense Death and Fire, he showed how powerfully he could express the darker side of his imagination.

99 'KIRCHEN AM BERG'/'Feder, aquarelliert, Schreibpapier/20.9:15.3/nicht signiert

Visual Arts Library/© ADAGP, Paris/COSMOPRESS, Geneva, 1988

The City of Churches *1918*
8″ × 6″ Private Collection

Klee found watercolour the perfect medium to convey light and clarity of atmosphere. Whether in figurative works or semi-abstract images (on opposite page), he used watercolour with freshness and directness to suggest shimmering heat and exotic colour, or simply the contrasting hues of a simple town view.

With The Eagle *1918*
6¾″ × 10″ Paul Klee Foundation,
Kunstmuseum, Berne

One of the most original features of Klee's work is the way in which he breaks free of traditional conventions of composition, which demand that a particular episode or part of the picture is the focus of attention. Here, as in so many of his works, he uses a free juxtaposition of forms to suggest the constant flux of nature – 'investing Creation with permanence', as he himself put it. The eagle is a bird rich in symbolic meaning; because of its keen eyes it was used, for example, as a personification of sight, and here it stands above an eye-like form, surveying the visual splendour of nature. The painting also illustrates Klee's idea that there was a natural community between all created things, as the branches of the fir trees echo the eagle's wings.

85 'MIT DEM ADLER' Aquarell auf Saturnrot, Ingres, Kreidegrundiert/17,3:25,6/signiert links unten/Paul Klee-Stiftung, Bern

232 'DER VOLLMOND' Gemälde, Ölfarben auf Ölgrund, Papier auf Karton/49:37/signiert links unten/Privatbesitz München

Full Moon *1919*
19¼″ × 14½″ Private Collection, Munich

This is one of the most elaborate and carefully constructed of Klee's oil paintings of this period. Natural and architectural forms (notably the window on the left) interlock in a complex, patchwork-like pattern, and although there is some suggestion of spatial depth, we are more aware of the surface animation. There is no human life, but the landscape seems alive with a mysterious energy.

The Twittering Machine *1922*
16¼″ × 12″ without margins Collection, The Museum of Modern Art, New York

Four bird-like creatures are shown perched on a branch that turns into a crank (on the right). Turn the handle and they will twitter. No artist exploited the humorous potential of the machine better than Klee, and here he wittily blurs the distinction between the mechanical and the living. The spindly but expressive forms show Klee's supreme mastery of draughtsmanship, and the economy of his line.

R5(85) 'FISCHZAUBER' Gemälde Öl und Aquarellfarben, gefirnisst, Nesseltuch auf Karton/77.89/signiert links unten

Fish Magic *1925*
30" × 38½" Louise and Walter Arensberg Collection,
Philadelphia Museum of Modern Art

*When he travelled in Italy as a young man, Klee had been
fascinated by the aquarium at Naples, and fish often figure
in his paintings. The teeming variety of marine life – the
myriad shapes and colours – formed a counterpart to his
own exceptionally fertile visual imagination. Apart from
the fish, the picture also features human-like figures (such
as the clown, bottom left), flowers, a clock and the sun
placed within the crescent of the moon. On the clock, Klee
has indicated the date of the painting by emphasizing the
numbers 1, 9, 2 and 5. The female figure at the bottom of
the picture (centre right) has two faces, like the Roman god
Janus who symbolized past and future. The theme of the
painting thus seems to be time or timelessness.*

Monument in a Fertile Country 1929
18½" × 12" Paul Klee Foundation, Kunstmuseum, Berne

Klee made a visit to Egypt in December 1928 and January 1929. His stay was fairly brief, but it made as great an impact on him as his momentous journey to Tunisia, and led to a series of pictures on Egyptian subjects. He was fascinated by various aspects of the country's ancient civilisation, especially by hieroglyphs, and was overwhelmed by the massive simplicity of Egyptian sculpture and architecture. The bold and uncluttered shapes in this watercolour reflect this influence. In their flatness, they also suggest the bright light and the immensity of the desert. The warm, earthy colours add to Klee's evocation of a hot desert land.

N1(41) 'MONUMENT IM FRUCHTLAND'. Aquarell, Ingres/Sonderclasse/46cm × 30.8cm/signiert rechts oben/Paul Klee Stiftung im Kunstmuseum, Bern

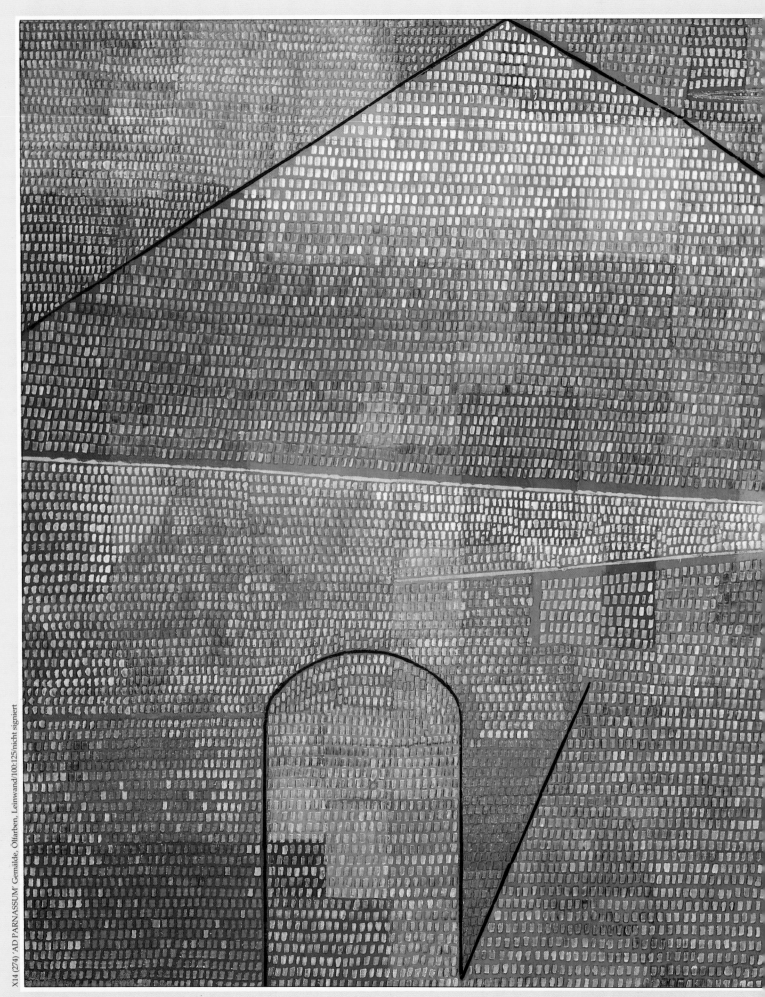

X14 (Z4) 'AD PARNASSUM' Gemälde, Ölfarben, Leinwand/100:125/nicht signiert

Ad Parnassum *1932*
39½″ × 49½″ Kunstmuseum, Berne

The title of this painting is said to derive from an 18th century musical treatise, Gradus ad Parnassum *(The Path to Parnassus), Parnassus being a mountain range in Greece that, in classical mythology, was sacred to the God Apollo and thus the traditional abode of music and poetry. The bold triangular shape represents the mountain, the red circle the sun, and the arched form at the bottom the portal of a temple. Klee himself was a skilled musician and here he seems to be trying to find a pictorial expression for the musical ideas of polyphony (the use of many voices) and counterpoint (the combining of different melodies), as contrasting shapes and varying hues are played off against each other within an overall visual harmony. This was Klee's largest painting up to this time, and the variegated, mosaic-like colours are set off against each other with a glorious resonance.*

F3 (343) 'FLORA AM FELSEN' Gemälde, Öl und Temperafarben, Jute/90·70/nicht signiert

© ADAGP, Paris/COSMOPRESS, Geneva, 1988

Rock Flora *1940*
35½″ × 27½″ Kunstmuseum, Berne

In the last years of his life, Klee's work took on a much more sombre cast, reflecting both his own illness and the dark historical events of the time. His forms became simpler and coarser, and he frequently used heavier outlines. There is often a feeling, as here, of a return from the sublime flights of fancy of his earlier work to weightier and more down-to-earth concerns.

G12 (332) 'TOD UND FEUER' Gemälde, Ölfarben, Jute, braun grundiert signiert rechts oben/46:44

Death and Fire *1940*

18½″ × 17½″ Paul Klee Foundation, Kunstmuseum, Berne

Even when he was facing death, Klee never lost his sense of fun, but in this profound work – one of the last he painted – it is grim and macabre humour. The features of the ghastly, ashen face, leering with malign triumph, are made up of the letters 'TOD' ('Tod' being German for 'death'), and the ultimate, terrifying mystery is concentrated into a few broad strokes of the brush.

Discovering the Unconscious

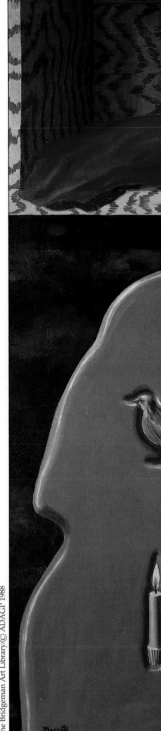

Though artists and poets have always drawn intuitively on the unconscious, Freud's scientific study of it at the turn of the last century was to prove revolutionary for all Western thought.

Images from the unconscious mind and memories of dreams have come to assume an important place in modern art. Yet it was not until the early years of this century, with the pioneering work of Sigmund Freud and his followers, that the hidden territory of the unconscious was first systematically explored. Ironically, it was in the deeply conservative, imperial capital of Vienna that Freud, a sober and respectable physician, developed his revolutionary theories of sexuality, and made his clinical study of neurotics the basis for a startling new view of human nature.

Freud was born into a cultivated, middle-class family at Freiburg in Moravia, which was then part of the Austrian Empire. When he was still a child, the family moved to Vienna, and Freud was later admitted to Vienna University to study medicine.

At this stage in his life, Freud was more attracted to pure research than clinical practice, but the need to make a living led him to join the staff of Vienna General Hospital as a physician. Contacts he made there stimulated his interest in the psychological aspects of nervous disorders. And so, abandoning his study of the nervous systems of crayfish, he turned his attentions to the neuroses of human beings instead.

Working with an older man, Josef Breuer, Freud became interested in the treatment of hysteria. In 1885-86 he studied under a famous French neurologist, Jean-Martin Charcot, at the Saltpetrière Hospital in Paris. Unlike most specialists, Charcot recognized that hysteria was not just 'imagination', but a striking manifestation of psychosomatic powers, involving phenomena

The Father of Psychoanalysis
(left) Freud spent most of his life in Vienna where he established a flourishing practice in spite of opposition to his revolutionary ideas on curing neuroses by psychoanalysis.

Male hysteria
(below) The theory of psychoanalysis was derived largely from Freud's studies of hysterical patients. In 1886, he published a paper refuting the idea that hysteria was a purely female complaint.

The Bridgeman Art Library/© ADAGP 1988

Tate Gallery

Mary Evans Picture Library

4   **Medicinischer Verlag von Franz Deuticke.**

Neue Vorlesungen über die
Krankheiten des Nervensystems
insbesondere über Hysterie.
Von **J. M. Charcot.**
Autorisirte deutsche Ausgabe von
Dr. Sigm. Freud,
Docent an der k. k. Universität in Wien.
Mit 59 Abbildungen.
1886. — Preis 9 M. Geb. M. 10.60.

Aus einem Falle männlicher Hysterie.

The logic of dreams
(left) The Surrealists readily adopted psychoanalytic theories. Magritte's The Reckless Sleeper *embodies the seeming irrationality of a dreamer's world – but Freud had shown that dreams can have their own logic.*

Kunsthalle, Bremen

such as the appearance of marks on the body and convincing phantom pregnancies. Charcot investigated his cases with the help of hypnotism, a technique then mostly regarded as fraudulent.

Charcot's work impressed Freud, who was also struck by one of the Frenchman's remarks – that behind every case of hysteria lay a sexual cause. However, when Freud lectured at the Vienna Medical Society on these topics, he met with a hostile reception. It was typical of the period that when Freud referred to male hysterics, he was assured that there was no such thing: hysteria, with its vaguely discreditable associations, was held to be a purely female affliction. Challenged to prove his point, Freud found an unmistakable case of male hysteria – but only after several weeks during which his search was hampered at every turn by obstructive hospital authorities.

In this unfavourable atmosphere, Freud stopped lecturing and worked on in isolation; even old friends like Breuer broke with him because of his increasing emphasis on sexual influences beginning in infancy. However, it was one of Breuer's patients, 'Anna O.', whose case led to Freud's greatest discovery. Under hypnosis, 'Anna' revealed memories of which her conscious mind was totally ignorant. The memories, said Freud, were imprisoned in the unconscious mind, where all the individual's recollections of damaging and painful experiences, known as traumata, were held.

Freud suggested that the conscious mind defended itself from such memories by repressing them and forcing them into the

Childhood trauma
(above) Munch was probably unaware of psychoanalytic theory, but his portrayal of mental anguish is unerring. In The Dead Mother, *he instinctively depicts the child's anxiety at a situation too unbearable to confront and which she literally tries to shut out. Such repression of early painful memories, Freud maintained, could often be the cause of neurotic behaviour in adult life.*

A new school of thought
(above and right) In 1900, Freud published his Interpretation of Dreams – *a milestone in the history of psychoanalysis as a distinct movement. By 1911, congresses, as this one in Weimar, were attracting distinguished adherents.*

unconscious. He argued that it was only under the influence of acute distress that these traumata were re-activated, when they manifested themselves in coded form; through hysteria, neuroses and obsessional behaviour. Freud's explanation of neurotic behaviour was revolutionary since it was generally held that the symptoms of neurotics were meaningless aberrations, totally irrelevant to the diagnosis of their maladies.

THE BIRTH OF PSYCHOANALYSIS

Freud went on to investigate the ways in which coded messages from the unconscious appeared in everyday life – in slips of the tongue, in jokes, and, above all, in dreams. He also devised a new technique for making contact with the unconscious. He abandoned hypnotism and encouraged the patient to say anything that came into his or her mind. During this 'free association', coded messages from the unconscious gradually emerged. The experienced analyst could decipher them and eventually persuade the patient to confront the trauma that lay at the root of his difficulties. The method of free association was central to what Freud called, 'psychoanalysis', and so was the conviction that cures could be effected

Disturbing sleep
(right) Long before Freud 'discovered' the unconscious, artists had shown its strange and often disquieting imagery in enigmatic paintings such as Fuseli's The Nightmare, *painted in 1781.*

widespread hostility, had acquired the closed, intolerant character of a persecuted religious sect. Freud himself became deeply attached to his most gifted disciples, but was prone to take offence at the slightest hint of dissent. Something of the atmosphere within the Freudian circle is conveyed by C. G. Jung's description of the religious solemnity with which Freud once said to him, 'My dear Jung, promise me never to abandon the sexual theory' – as if the sexual theory were a fixed moral law.

HERESIES AND SCHISMS

This attitude made it inevitable that dissenters would be driven out of the orthodox movement, and would therefore elaborate their heresies into rival systems. There were several defections even before the First World War. Alfred Adler was drummed out in 1911 and developed his theory of Individual Psychology, based on the idea that feelings of inferiority were created by childhood weakness (the famous 'inferiority complex') and that this created the drive for power or domination. For Adler, sex was one possible expression of the power drive, not vice versa. In the long run, C. G. Jung, who had defected by 1914, was even more influential. His classification of personalities into introverts and extroverts has entered ordinary speech and his theory that beneath the personal unconscious there lies the collective unconscious of humanity full of 'archetypal' symbolic figures is also well known. Jung's belief that this shared unconscious unites all cultures and finds expression in the world's myths, religions and works of art, had important repercussions for several painters, including Klee.

Michael Holford

A perfect symbol
(above) Jungian theories lay great stress on the meaning of symbols. A mandala – used in Buddhist meditation – signifies self-realization.

The favourite son
(below right) Though adopted by Freud as his professional heir, Jung had to break the bond when he developed incompatible ideas.

only by the catharsis of self-knowledge.

Freud gradually elaborated his theories into an all-embracing explanation of human behaviour. He suggested that the impulse of every human being to fulfil his or her sexual drives and desires was constantly thwarted by society. This resulted in traumata which were pushed into the unconscious, while the drives themselves were re-channelled or 'sublimated' into socially acceptable goals. In the Freudian scheme of things, all human achievement and culture – including all artistic activity – represented a sublimation of more direct and primitive urges.

To Freud – himself a highly cultivated man – this was the hard but inescapable truth about human life. His followers, however, did not all agree with him that sex was the sole motivating force in mankind's behaviour. By the time he was in his fifties, Freud's publications had earned him an international reputation, and a number of disciples. There was Alfred Adler in Vienna, Karl Abraham in Germany, C. G. Jung in Switzerland, and Ernest Jones in Britain.

However, those who doubted Freud in any way found themselves in an awkward position. The psychoanalytical movement, having faced a

Musee Guimet, Paris

Bildarchiv Preussischer Kulturbesitz

A Year in the Life 1933

Klee left Germany in 1933, shortly after Hitler took power. By this time, the rise of Fascism and the effects of the Depression had created tensions and conflicts on an international scale. One solution, the 'New Deal', was introduced by the new President of the United States, F. D. Roosevelt.

Adolf Hitler became Chancellor of Germany on 30 January. Although his Nazi party was the most powerful in Germany, backed by a private army of SA and SS troops, it did not have a majority in the Reichstag (German parliament). Hitler had been called in when the dominant right-wing politicians fell out among themselves. They believed they could control Hitler, since they allowed the Nazis to hold only one other important cabinet seat, but they had badly miscalculated.

Within weeks, the Reichstag Fire gave impetus to Hitler's 'Red Threat' propaganda. At the time, people on the Left accused the Nazis of starting the fire themselves, but it now seems more likely that they cleverly exploited this act of arson by a crazed Dutchman. In new elections during March, with the police and media under their control, the Nazis greatly

The Reichstag Fire
(left) A little after nine o'clock on the evening of 27 February, the German government building burst into flames. A Dutchman, van der Lubbe, was accused of arson, but the Nazi leadership cunningly maintained that the fire was a Communist plot. Overnight, Goering organised a massive round-up of not only Communists, but socialists, pacifist writers, doctors and lawyers – in fact anyone considered hostile to the new regime. The following day, President Hindenburg signed an Enabling Act giving Hitler dictatorial powers 'to protect the nation from the Communist danger'.

Archiv für Kunst und Geschichte

British Film Institute

improved their vote. A deal with the Catholic Centre Party provided them with the majority they needed to pass an Enabling Act giving Hitler dictatorial powers for four years. Within as many months, the new, legally constituted dictator had suppressed trade unions and political parties, and transformed the Weimar Republic into the Third Reich. Hitler's reign of unparalleled political terrorism had started.

FASCISM TO THE FORE

By 1933, Fascism was on the march. There were Fascist parties and parliamentary groups in most countries from Finland to Latin America – even in Ireland, where General Duffy's Blue Shirts reached the peak of their influence. In December 1933,

the French business empire of a Russian-born Jewish swindler named Serge Alexandre Stavisky collapsed; in 1934 his activities and connections would provide Fascists and monarchists alike with powerful ammunition to use against the corrupt politicians of the Third Republic. Austria dissolved its Nazi Party and seemed safe for the moment. But in Czechoslovakia, the large German minority was already restive; the Nazi Party there dissolved itself before the government could move against it, reforming as the nominally more law-abiding Sudeten German Party. In response to the rise of Fascism, intellectuals began to swing to the Left, although pacifism remained strong for some years in England, where the Oxford Union passed a celebrated motion that 'This house would refuse to fight for king and country'.

The real face of National Socialism
(below) This uncompromising American cartoon of 1933 depicting Hitler as Death armed with scythes in the shape of a swastika was also prophetic. The Nazi leader who had engineered his own rise to power with a cleverly orchestrated reign of terror was about to re-arm and sow destruction beyond the borders of Germany.

Giancarlo Costa

End of Prohibition
(above) President Roosevelt, anxious to deal with the problems of the Depression, repealed the Eighteenth Amendment which had become federal law in 1920, remarking, 'I think that this would be a good time for beer'. It spelt the end of the era of bootleggers and speakeasies, but 13 years of Prohibition had changed the face of America. Crime had become big business and the Bureau of Investigation (now the FBI) under J. Edgar Hoover had expanded rapidly to deal with the menace.

Lovable monster
(left) RKO's celebrated adventure film King Kong *went on the cinema circuits after its première on 2 March 1933, backed by a massive publicity campaign. This included stunts such as 30-foot food wagons labelled, 'Just one breakfast for Kong!' and cages of small monkeys carrying signs reading, 'We are the degenerate descendants of the mighty Kong!' In reality, the new film star was a mere 18 inches tall, the fearsome product of a brilliant special effects team. Little did they or RKO studio executives guess that in the brutal Kong, humanised by his hopeless love for the helpless Fay Wray, they had created a latter-day cult hero.*

Archiv für Kunst und Geschichte

73

Economic hardship was an important reason for Fascist successes, and in 1933, the Great Depression continued its savage course. In January, the United States had a new president who pledged to introduce a 'New Deal' to cope with the Depression. By American standards, Franklin D. Roosevelt's programme was a radical one. Dealings in securities were tightened to prevent any repetition of the Wall Street Crash. Provision was made for emergency relief for the hard-hit. The mortgages of home-buyers were re-financed. New credits and the regulation of production helped farmers, and new public works schemes such as the Tennessee Valley project ultimately produced employment for millions of people. However, the most popular of all the administration's actions was probably the passing of the 21st Amendment to the Constitution – the repeal of Prohibition.

The year 1933 was turbulent in many parts of the world. President Roosevelt announced a 'good neighbour' policy of non-intervention in Latin America . . . and US warships were sent to Cuba, where power was eventually seized by Fulgencio Batista, who maintained almost unbroken control of the island until Fidel Castro's victory in 1958. A parliamentary committee drafted a constitution for India but at the same time Gandhi was sentenced to twelve months' imprisonment. English 'bodyline' bowling in cricket strained Anglo-Australian relations. Western Australia voted to secede from the Australian Commonwealth. And, in a curious historical step backwards, debt-ridden Newfoundland was deprived of her Dominion status and became a Crown Colony.

Roosevelt and the New Deal
(left and below) Franklin D. Roosevelt was inaugurated President of the United States on 4 March 1933, the same day as the banks of Chicago and New York, twin centres of American capitalism, were closed down. However, unlike his predecessor, Roosevelt was determined to face the national misery and disaster inflicted by the Great Depression. True to his promise of 'I pledge you, I pledge myself, to a new deal for the American people', he set up numerous projects during his four terms as president to achieve financial recovery and the relief of unemployment through work and social security measures. Perhaps most important, he gave hope to millions.

Giancarlo Costa

Archiv für Kunst und Geschichte

74

MARC CHAGALL

1887-1985

Marc Chagall is one of the greatest and most popular European painters of the 20th century. Born into a humble Jewish family in the Russian town of Vitebsk, he escaped the confines of provincial life by travelling first to St Petersburg, and then to Paris, in search of an artistic education. Yet although France became Chagall's adopted homeland, his art always retained a strong Russian and Jewish identity.

Memories of peasant life recur constantly in Chagall's work, but they are transformed by his poetic vision into free-floating dream images that are juxtaposed in a surprising and highly original manner. Chagall's output was prodigious, for in addition to his imaginative paintings he illustrated books, made ceramics, and designed theatre sets and mosaics. He was also one of the finest modern stained glass artists.

The Jewish Emigré

Throughout his long life, Chagall turned to his Russo-Jewish background for inspiration. His happy marriage with Bella, too, was reflected in his images of brides and couples.

Ginette Laborde, Paris Charenton, France

school, Chagall decided that he wanted to become an artist, although it was hardly a profession with which he was familiar. He eventually left school and summoned up the courage to call on the local artist Jehuda Pen to ask for lessons. Pen looked at his sketches, and immediately set Chagall the task of drawing from plaster casts. Chagall did not stay with Pen for very long, as one of his classmates soon convinced him that a period of study in St Petersburg was far more essential to his artistic education. He began an apprenticeship as a photographer's retoucher, which he abandoned in 1906, and after a furious argument with his father who was dismayed at his foolhardiness, he fled to the Russian capital with only a few roubles.

LIVING IN THE CITY

Jews were not supposed to live in St Petersburg unless their profession made it absolutely necessary, and Chagall had to indulge in an elaborate charade with the authorities to hide the fact that he did not have an official residence permit. At first he pretended to be a business representative for the merchants of Vitebsk, and

Marc Chagall entered the world amid great drama and excitement on 7 July 1887. At the moment of his birth in the Russian town of Vitebsk, a fire broke out in a nearby building, and mother and baby had to be carried to a safer part of town.

Almost half of Vitebsk's 60,000 inhabitants were Jewish, and the Chagall family were devout Hassidic Jews. Chagall's father – whom the artist later likened to 'one of those men in Florentine painting with an untrimmed beard, eyes that are brown and ash grey, and a complexion of burnt ochre furrowed with lines and wrinkles' – was a fishmonger's assistant who struggled to support ten children on his meagre wages. But Chagall never went hungry, and his humble circumstances did not prevent him from enjoying life. Relatives and elders at the synagogue ensured that the young boy was taught to play the violin and given singing lessons, and from an early age he drew pictures and wrote poems. Chagall's mother was quite ambitious for her son, and she bribed a schoolmaster to get him into a school that did not normally admit Jews, thinking that a reasonable education might enable him to rise above his father's lowly occupation and become a clerk.

However, it soon became apparent that she was going to be disappointed. While he was still at

Scenes from childhood
(above) Chagall's childhood in and around Vitebsk gave him a memory bank of images from which he drew all his life. Although Vitebsk was a bustling town with a large Jewish population, and the family lived in a suburb of wooden houses with animals in the back yards, Chagall had memories of the countryside too – from summers spent in a nearby village with his grandfather.

Student of art
(right) Chagall first studied with Jehuda Pen, a traditional Salon painter unaffected by Russian avant-garde interest in folk motifs and icons.

Edimages

Marc Chagall

Key Dates

1887 born in Vitebsk

1906-10 studies in St Petersburg

1910 moves to Paris

1914 travels to Berlin for one-man show then returns to Vitebsk

1915 marries Bella Rosenfeld

1916 birth of Ida

1918 appointed Commissar for the Arts in Vitebsk

1920 moves to Moscow

1923 returns to Paris and begins work on etchings

1939 moves to the south of France

1941 goes to New York and works on ballet designs

1944 death of Bella

1948 permanently returns to France

1950 moves to Vence; takes up ceramics and stained glass

1952 marries Valentina Brodsky

1985 dies at Saint-Paul

La Ruche
(below) This Pavilion of Wines from the Universal Exhibition of 1900 became a hive of studies for poor artists. The iron gateway came from the Exhibition's Palace of Women.

A teacher's example
(above) In St Petersburg, Chagall studied with Léon Bakst, a Jew with similar origins to himself. Bakst was known for his designs for the Ballets Russes' Schéhérazade, and, as described by Chagall, his painting was 'refined and sometimes decadent'. Chagall learnt little from Bakst himself, but at his studio he was exposed to Symbolism and other avant-garde influences which had originated in Paris.

later he claimed to be a footman in a wealthy Jewish household, but this did not prevent him being thrown into gaol on one occasion. Too poor to afford a room of his own, Chagall rented an alcove in a room with several others. In an attempt to obtain a regular craftsman's permit and some money, he apprenticed himself to a signwriter, but the prospect of sitting the lettering exams appalled him, and he quickly abandoned this second apprenticeship.

In spite of his hardship, Chagall did manage to embark on his artistic training. He started off at the School of the Imperial Society for the Protection of Fine Art, but soon found that the teaching there bored him, and that the atmosphere was depressing. 'It was cold in the classrooms', he complained, 'the smell of damp combined with the smell of clay paints, pickle and cabbage and

Friends in Paris

The painters Robert and Sonia Delaunay played an important part in Chagall's life during his first stay in Paris. Sonia, who was herself Russian, made a point of befriending fellow Russian artists and inviting them to her social gatherings on Sunday afternoons, and Chagall even stayed at the couple's country house in the summer of 1913. At the time, the Delaunays were at the head of a new development in French painting which Apollinaire called 'Orphism' – a name derived from Orpheus, the poet of Greek mythology. Orphist artists wanted to reintroduce poetry and colour into Cubism to create a more lyrical kind of art, an aim with which Chagall was entirely in agreement. The lighter colours and the more harmonious and unified compositions that he began to employ around this date owed a great deal to the example of the Delaunays.

The City of Paris (1910)
(right) Robert Delaunay's use of Cubist form and his lyrical colour sense influenced Chagall. Delaunay was the first artist to use the Eiffel Tower in his work as a symbol of modern civilization.

stagnant water in the Moyky Canal.'

Having endured two years in this environment, Chagall enrolled at the Zvantseva School run by Léon Bakst, 'the only school animated by the breath of Europe,' where he found himself sharing a studio with Tolstoy's daughter Vera, and the dancer Nijinsky. The Zvantseva School was more lively than anything that Chagall had known previously, and he spent two years under Bakst's tutelage.

THE MOVE TO PARIS

In 1910, Bakst announced that he was going to Paris to join Diaghilev's Ballets Russes as a designer, and it was not long before Chagall made up his mind that he should go to Paris too. As luck would have it, he found that the Jewish lawyer Max Vinaver, who had bought two of his paintings, was prepared to pay his fare and give him a monthly allowance to study in the city, so he set off in the autumn of that year.

The light, the streets and the people of Paris were an instant inspiration to Chagall. He also found in the paintings that hung on the walls of the Louvre and in the Salon des Indépendants what he called a 'painterly' kind of painting; a feeling for proportion, clarity and form that he had always felt was missing in Russian art. In 1912, Chagall moved to a studio in the building called La Ruche ('the bee-hive'), near the Vaugirard slaughterhouses, which was occupied by artistic bohemians from all over the world. The place hummed with activity: 'While offended models sobbed in Russian studios, Italian ones rang with

Amedeo Modigliani: Portrait of Blaise Cendrars

song and Jewish ones with discussion', Chagall wrote in his autobiography. He enjoyed the company, but immersed himself in work, usually painting through the night. He lived on hot rolls bought on credit, herrings, and two-sou jars of soup, praying that someone would take him out to lunch occasionally.

Chagall worked in a frenzy of excitement. There were so many new ideas to assimilate, from the achievements of the Cubists to the experiments with colour and form that his friends, the

Blaise Cendrars
(left) This lively poet-adventurer befriended Chagall. He greatly admired Chagall's blend of fantasy and fact in his work.

Mauro Pucciarelli

Musée Nationale d'Art Moderne, Paris

Delaunays, were carrying out. Chagall was sustained through this period of change and challenge by the encouragement offered by the two poets Blaise Cendrars and Guillaume Apollinaire, who both assured the young artist of the excellence of his original and expressive manner of painting and who celebrated his talent in their poems. Chagall painted at a prodigious rate, and the canvases piled up against the walls of his studio. He began to send pictures to the Salon des Indépendants, and to avant-garde exhibitions in Russia, but he did not manage to sell much.

RETURN TO RUSSIA

In 1914, it seemed as though recognition was about to arrive when Herwath Walden, the editor of the German magazine *Der Sturm*, offered Chagall an exhibition in his magazine's headquarters in Berlin. In May that year, Chagall travelled with most of his paintings to Berlin to hang the exhibition. Since Vitebsk seemed enticingly near, and the artist wanted to go back for his sister's wedding and to see the sweetheart he had left behind five years previously, he returned to his native town that summer. The outbreak of war in August meant that Chagall's Russian holiday was to be prolonged for an indefinite period.

The year after his return to Russia, Chagall married his fiancée Bella Rosenfeld, but not before there had been harsh words from her parents, prominent citizens of Vitebsk, who felt that the fresh-faced and rather whimsical young artist would never be able to support a family. For the next thirty years, Bella was to be Chagall's muse and critic. The couple enjoyed a period of idyllic happiness following their wedding and the birth of their daughter Ida in 1916, and Chagall began to paint closely observed pictures of his home town and its inhabitants, as well as his new bride. Although he had to endure a spell of military service as an office clerk in St Petersburg, Chagall still managed to find the time to paint.

A more severe disruption came with the outbreak of the Russian Revolution in 1917. Chagall was not a man of strong political opinions, but he instinctively felt the importance of the upheaval, and was drawn into events almost in spite of himself. In 1918, he was appointed Commissar of Art for Vitebsk and the surrounding region, and put in charge of an art school, a museum, and theatre production. Although he was an energetic organizer, Chagall did not altogether enjoy his new role. He found it dispiriting to attempt to negotiate money for his art

Chagall's wife and model

(below) Chagall married Bella Rosenfeld in 1915 in Vitebsk. It was a love-match which lasted until her sudden death in 1944, leaving Chagall devastated. Bella was his soul-mate and only model. Their happiness is celebrated in the numerous paintings of lovers and brides that he painted throughout his life.

Spectrum Colour Library

Brittany's Emerald Coast

(above) In the 1920s, Chagall discovered the French countryside, where he spent long periods. The light and landscape delighted him and influenced his painting style, bringing about a much softer treatment.

school from the Soviets, and he was profoundly distressed when Malevich arrived at the Vitebsk School of Art and stirred up rebellion against him and his teaching methods. Disillusioned with the whole experience, Chagall fled to Moscow in 1920 to face a terrible winter of hardship with no work. Eventually, commissions to decorate two Moscow theatres and an invitation from the state to teach war orphans in nearby children's colonies, rescued him from penury.

Chagall returned to Paris after a nine-year-

79

A New Beginning

During the 1950s, following his establishment of a permanent home in Provence and marriage to Vava, Chagall embarked upon a new period of artistic experimentation. He became increasingly interested in public decorative schemes, and as easel painting came to occupy a less important place in his art, he began to make ceramics and design mosaics and stained glass. Chagall's first attempt at stained glass came in 1957 when he was invited to decorate the baptistery of Notre Dame at Assy. Following this modest start, he was commissioned to create his first stained glass windows at Metz Cathedral. This marked the beginning of a long collaboration between Chagall and the glassmaker, Charles Marq of Reims, who skilfully translated the artist's paintings into glass. An enormous number of commissions from religious and secular institutions from all over the world soon followed, and Chagall rapidly became one of the most highly regarded stained glass artists of modern times.

The Photo Source

A public figure
(right) This photograph shows Chagall at the age of 82 at the opening of his exhibition at the Grand Palais in Paris; with him is the French Prime Minister. From the 1950s, Chagall increasingly changed his artistic direction and his success with ceramics and stained glass windows brought him commissions which put him firmly within the public eye. His wife, Vava, managed his affairs, leaving him free to get on with his work.

Louis-Yves Loirant/Explorer/© ADAGP 1988

Windows in Jerusalem
(left) In 1959, Chagall was given a commission which touched him deeply – to design windows for the synagogue of the university clinic in Jerusalem. They show the 12 tribes of Israel, each window representing a tribe. Because ancient Jewish tradition forbade images of man, Chagall used symbols to portray the character of each tribe. Here the green window shows symbols of war, denoting the warrior tribe, Gad, while the blue window of Dan shows the peaceful light of the candelabra.

absence in 1923, only to find that his paintings had disappeared from his La Ruche studio. However, the news that the art dealer Ambroise Vollard wanted him to do a series of etchings to illustrate Gogol's *Dead Souls* brought some optimism for the future. A further commission to illustrate La Fontaine's *Fables* followed in 1927, followed by a request for a series of illustrations for the Bible in 1930. Chagall particularly enjoyed this last commission as it gave him the opportunity to travel to Palestine, Egypt and Syria to gain a first-hand impression of the Holy Land, as well as Holland to see the Biblical paintings of Rembrandt, and Spain to see El Greco's works.

By the 1930s, Chagall was the subject of worldwide fame and admiration, but his personal good fortune was set against a backdrop of growing political turbulence in Europe, where the rapid rise to power of the Nazis and civil strife in Spain presented a bleak outlook. In 1933, Goebbels ordered some of Chagall's paintings to be burnt in Mannheim, and the mood of gloom and despondency that crept into paintings such as *Solitude* (pp.94-5) and *White Crucifixion* during this period reflects the artist's concern with the fate of his fellow human beings. In 1939, shortly before the outbreak of the Second World War, the Chagalls moved to the South of France.

Exile in America
(left) When the Germans occupied France, Chagall decided to leave with his family. They emigrated to America, arriving on 23 June 1941 – the day the Nazis invaded Russia. As an exile in New York, Chagall felt most at home on the Jewish Lower East Side and his friends were mainly Russian-Jewish emigrés like himself. Never at ease in New York, the Chagalls eagerly awaited the fall of Paris, so they could return to France. Sadly, Bella died suddenly before they could leave.

The following year, anxious to escape the relentless Nazi advance through France, Chagall accepted an invitation from the Museum of Modern Art in New York to leave for the US.

A series of commissions for theatrical and ballet designs kept Chagall busy during the war years, but just before peace was declared, fresh disaster struck with the sudden death of Bella. Grief-stricken, Chagall stopped painting for months, and it was his long affair with Virginia Haggard (who bore him a son, David) and an invitation to design the costumes and sets for an American production of Stravinsky's *The Firebird* that helped him out of his depression.

In 1947, Chagall felt it was safe to return to France, and after an initial period in Paris, he went back to the south and made his home in Vence, although he moved to the nearby village of Saint-Paul in 1966. The move back to France, and marriage to Valentine Brodsky, whom he nicknamed 'Vava', heralded a new era of stability and happiness in Chagall's life. The artist began to devote more and more time to the applied arts.

CHAGALL'S LATER WORK

Commissions flooded in from all over the world for stained glass windows, monumental paintings and tapestries. Chagall presided over his craftsmen, glass-makers, mosaicists and weavers like the master of a vast Renaissance workshop, and managed to complete a variety of large projects ranging from stained glass windows for the Cathedrals of Rheims and Metz and the synagogue at the Hadassah-Hebrew University in Jerusalem, tapestries for the Israeli Knesset, and a mosaic ceiling for the Paris Opéra. He also found

time to experiment with ceramics – the region of Vence is renowned for its pottery.

The work which probably meant most to Chagall was, however, the 17 canvases that made up his *Biblical Message,* housed in a small building on a hillside above Nice which opened in 1973. It was intended as a haven for meditation; a reflection of the artist's desire for peace after the turbulent times he had lived through.

Chagall died in 1985, just as his major retrospective was closing in London. He was buried in the cemetery at Saint-Paul.

Vence
(below) The pottery centre of Vence where Chagall lived inspired him to work with ceramics. He was attracted by the radiance of colour shining through the glaze. He decorated and, later, modelled his own vases and plaques.

The Mirror of Memory

Although influenced by current avant-garde artistic trends, Chagall pursued a highly individual style with images often derived from childhood memories, and a distinctive use of colour.

'The soil that nourished the roots of my art was Vitebsk', Chagall wrote in his autobiography, 'but my art desired Paris as a tree desires water.' It is significant that the artist named places rather than artists as his source of inspiration, because although he came under the influence of the Post-Impressionists, the Fauves, the Cubists and the Surrealists at various stages during his career, Chagall's art does not really belong to any of these movements. He always preferred to develop his individual vision in his own way, and blended the

real and the imaginary, and flouted laws of time, space and gravity in his canvases to create his highly personal fantasy world.

The pictures that Chagall painted during his student days in St Petersburg are bold, naive depictions of his family and village which owe something to the example of Gauguin, whom he greatly admired at the time. Although they contain distortions of anatomy and perspective, the paintings are still firmly rooted in observable reality. Chagall had, however, already begun to

My Fiancée with Black Gloves (1909)
(right) Chagall has here portrayed his wife-to-be in an unusual pose; by contrasting her black gloved hands against a white dress, he has stressed the expressive nature of her stance.
It is possible that the unusual pose may have been influenced by one of the drawings for a contemporary Russian stage production. These depended upon the use of strong silhouette, which was achieved by outlining the costumes, for their major impact.

The Poet Reclining (1915)
(above) This is one of Chagall's most tranquil paintings where man, animals and nature are at peace together in total harmony. The reclining figure is that of Chagall himself, resting his head on his palette. A possible source of inspiration for this work may have been Hassidic philosophy.

Kunstmuseum, Basle

82

and not a suitable subject for dry scientific analysis. 'Let them choke themselves on their square pears on their triangular tables', he wrote about the Cubists. 'My art is an extravagant art, a flaming vermilion, a blue soul flooding over my paintings.' Although works such as *I and the Village* (p.85) show a clear debt to Cubism in their pictorial arrangement, the harmony of image and colour always prevails over the actual structure of the picture. It is also likely that Chagall found an additional source of inspiration to Cubism for his dislocations of time and space, in Russian icons: these often portray events that occurred at separate times and in different places, in small compartments within the same picture.

When Chagall returned to Paris after the First World War, he was confronted with a new development in painting – Surrealism. Many of the central concerns of the new movement – the importance of the subconscious, dream imagery, and the apparently illogical juxtapositions of objects – were preoccupations that Chagall shared. But he found himself unable to fully share their emphasis on the supremacy of individual experience at the expense of universal themes.

Chagall's work was certainty rooted in his own experience, and he used images of peasants, animals, musicians, Jews and lovers drawn from his own life, but he wanted them to convey universal emotions, not feelings that were peculiar to himself. It is probably this strong wish that his pictures should surpass their purely autobiographical content that accounts for

use colour in a bizarre and distinctive manner, for he tells us in his autobiography that he painted a series of 'violet' pictures while he was still a young boy in his teens.

The artist's first encounter with the work of the Cubists on his move to Paris in 1910 was both a revelation and a source of frustration. On the one hand, Cubist pictures were exciting because they broke with the tradition of realism in art, but on the other hand, their range of subject matter was very limited. Chagall himself never found still-lifes very interesting, and he was constantly dismayed by the Cubist tendency towards abstraction. For him, painting was a reflection of the state of the soul,

The Fiddler (1912-13)
(right) A familiar figure in rural Russian life, the fiddler often recurs in Chagall's art and this is one of his finest representations of the theme.

Stedelijk Museum, Amsterdam/© ADAGP 1988

Tate Gallery, London

Images of Fantasy

The element of fantasy so prominent in Chagall's art is largely derived from his own experiences, memories and dreams. Fantasy images have always existed in art but have usually been clothed in mythological guise. However, in the 19th century – probably as a reaction to prevailing naturalistic conventions – fantasy came to play a much larger role in painting. Artists invented their own personal myths to express their inner lives and reinterpreted mythological themes.

Richard Dadd (1819-87) **The Fairy Feller's Master Stroke**
(left) Dadd is famous for his fairy subjects, which he painted while confined to a lunatic asylum for murdering his father.

Gustave Moreau (1826-98) **The Unicorns**
(detail right) Moreau's scene shows unicorns, mythic symbols of chastity associated with virgins.

Réunion des Musée Nationaux

Musée Gustave Moreau, Paris

Chagall's remarkable reluctance to explain his symbolism in words, or to allow anyone else to do so for him.

When questioned about the recurrence of certain familiar images in his work, Chagall simply said that he used cows, girls, cocks and the houses of provincial Russia as his fundamental forms because they belonged to his childhood and had obviously made a deep impact upon his visual memory. But he wanted them to be seen as pieces in the jigsaw of an entire composition, and not subjected to an over-specific interpretation.

CHAGALL'S SYMBOLISM

In any case, Chagall's subjects should not always be taken at face value, as the artist sometimes used symbols to mean the exact opposite of what one might imagine. On being asked about his love of images of the circus and acrobats, he explained: 'I have always regarded clowns, acrobats and actors as tragic figures, which for me resemble the figures in certain religious paintings. I did not want to spare any of the more moving, tender feelings in a picture of a clown or a circus rider, feelings which one would experience in painting a Madonna, a Christ . . . or a pair of lovers. One could enlarge this idea and

say that a so-called "subject" . . . should not, in fact, exactly resemble that which it intends to express, but rather make an allusion to something else in order to achieve that resemblance.'

That Chagall was aiming for universality in his art through his subtle use of symbolism is most obvious in his Biblical pictures, which cannot be tied to any one creed. Although he was a Jew, the Christian image of the Crucifixion was for him a potent image of suffering that could be used to embrace the whole of humanity, as can be seen in *White Crucifixion*.

Just as Chagall's pictures cannot be neatly categorized as belonging to any one art movement, so his work defies any attempt to trace a precise chronological sequence of artistic evolution. Chagall often worked on the same picture for decades, and similar images and preoccupations recur throughout his life. Generally speaking, it is true to say that the forms in his paintings become less sharply defined, and more submerged in broad sweeps of colour as he grew older, but presented as a whole, Chagall's work is remarkably unified. It is the expression of a profoundly original personality; of a man who had become a painter because painting 'seemed to me like a window through which I could have taken flight to another world.'

I and the Village

This picture was painted in 1911, after Chagall arrived in Paris, and shows how he adapted Cubism to his own ends. Conventional three-dimensional perspective has been abandoned in favour of an ambiguous depiction of space, and the forms seem more transparent than solid. Chagall's love of brilliant colour applied in an unnaturalistic manner is also evident. The disparate images drawn from memories of his native village are bound together by the geometrical arrangement of diagonals, circles and curves on the picture surface. The man with the green face represents the artist himself. He stares intently at the white cow – a symbol of rural security – while clutching a flowering twig, which possibly represents the tree of life. In contrast (detail below), is a man with a scythe – emblematic of death. In the background, are the buildings of Vitebsk.

6' 3⅝" × 59⅝"/oil on canvas

Mrs Simon Guggenheim Fund/© ADAGP 1988

Collection, The Museum of Modern Art, New York

> 'For me a picture is a surface covered with representations . . . in which logic and illustration have no importance.'
>
> Chagall

© ADAGP 1988

detail: I and the Village

Floating Forms

A characteristic feature of Chagall's art is that his figures and objects seldom stand firmly on the ground but are shown to float in space, giving them a dream-like quality. Conventional methods of defining space were unimportant to Chagall; his skies are peopled with seemingly unconnected images such as fiddlers, cows, garlands, candles and angels.

Gallery

Marc Chagall created a completely personal style based on two extremely rich sources of imagery: memories of Jewish life and folklore in his native Russia, and the Bible. His prismatic use of colour and some of his spatial effects reflect modern developments such as Cubism, but he attached himself to no single movement and was essentially one

Self-Portrait with Seven Fingers *1912*
49½″ × 42¼″ Stedelijk Museum, Amsterdam

The seven fingers of the painter's left hand are probably a reference to Jewish symbolism (one of the traditional emblems of Judaism being a seven-branched candelabra). In this startlingly unconventional self-portrait, Chagall combines his two worlds – Paris seen through the window, and Russia portrayed on his easel and in his 'vision' above.

of the most individual figures in 20th-century art. Paintings such as To Russia, Asses and Others often defy specific analysis, so unconventional is their imagery, and even autobiographical works such as The Birthday take on the appearance of a fairy-tale fantasy. Chagall himself said, 'I work with no express symbols, but, as it were, subconsciously.

When the picture is finished everyone can interpret it as he wishes.' But in spite of his avoidance of traditional religious imagery, Chagall's work often conveys a strong sense of the divine, as in Over Vitebsk and Solitude, and in his stained glass designs he proved himself one of the 20th century's great masters of the art.

To Russia, Asses and Others *1912* 61½″ × 48″ Musée National d'Art Moderne, Paris

Chagall is seen working on this picture (dated 1911 but painted in 1912) in the self-portrait opposite. One of the first pictures that he painted after moving to his studio at La Ruche, Chagall took the unusual title from his friend, the poet Blaise Cendrars. The strange juxtaposition of images is typical of his work: the main figure is a milkmaid whose head has become detached from her body, seeming to linger behind her striding form to gaze in wonder at the heavens.

Over Vitebsk *1914*
28¾″ × 36½″ Art Gallery of Ontario, Toronto

This is the first of several versions Chagall made of this subject. The picture gives a reasonably accurate and naturalistic view of the Iltych church in Chagall's native Vitebsk, so the huge figure that has emerged from over the horizon strikes an unexpected note and the meaning to be attached to him is a matter of debate. He has been connected with a Yiddish expression 'he walks over the city', describing a beggar who goes from door to door and who can be seen as symbolizing the persecution and discrimination that Jews in eastern Europe often met. However, as the figure seems benign and untroubled and the mood of the picture is certainly not gloomy or pessimistic, some critics feel that he represents the prophet Elijah, who in certain Jewish communities was supposed to appear in times of want, bearing gifts for the needy and deserving.

The Birthday *(1915)*
31¾″ × 39¼″ Collection, The Museum of
Modern Art, New York

*The two figures in this joyous painting are Chagall and
his future wife Bella, who is seen bringing him flowers
on his birthday. A pair of happy lovers was one of
Chagall's favourite themes, but he never surpassed the
ecstatic spirit conveyed here, showing himself twisting
rapturously in the air as he bends to kiss his beloved. The
mood of absurdity is wholly captivating and appropriate
to Bella's own account of the occasion: 'Through the
window a cloud and a patch of blue sky called to us. The
brightly hung walls whirled around us. We flew over
fields of flowers, shuttered houses, roofs, yards,
churches.'*

The Acrobat *1930*
25⅝″ × 20½″ Musée National d'Art Moderne, Paris

*In common with many other painters of the School of Paris, Chagall
found that the circus offered an abundance of colourful subjects. At the
time he painted this picture, he was highly successful and enjoying the
cosmopolitan social life of Paris; its buoyant charm reflects his newly
found sense of well-being.*

Equestrienne *1931*
39½″ × 31¾″ Stedelijk Museum, Amsterdam

Here Chagall introduces his favourite theme of young lovers into a circus setting. The horsewoman is a beautiful, graceful figure, and the picture has the air of a fairy-tale elopement. The smudged quality of the paint enhances the feeling of unreality, as does the horse holding the garlanded violin against its neck.

Solitude *1933*
40" × 66" The Tel-Aviv Museum

Chagall visited Palestine in 1931 to gain background experience before undertaking a commission to illustrate the Bible and this reflective work seems like a comment on his stay. Characteristically, Chagall does not use straightforward symbols in a conventional way, but he seems here to be expressing the longing of the pious Jew for faraway Israel. The massive, huddled figure clutching a Torah scroll is one of the most memorable in Chagall's work as is the placid-looking cow, which perhaps alludes to the idea of the innocent victim. Chagall himself presented this picture to the Tel Aviv Museum.

Bouquet with Flying Lovers *c.1934-47*
51½″ × 38½″ Tate Gallery, London

Chagall worked on this picture intermittently over a number of years, changing the composition several times. At the time when he completed it, Chagall was in mourning for his wife who died in 1944. He said it was one of the works that most expressed his feelings of loss and nostalgia. The woman, indeed, resembles a spirit in a bridal dress.

The Three Candles *1938-40*
51¼″ × 38″ Collection: The Readers Digest Association Inc.
Pleasantville, New York

*As in the picture on the opposite page, Chagall here combines the
themes of lovers and flowers. The candle is a symbol of faith,
appropriate as the couple are a bride and groom who seem bewildered
at the start of their new lives together.*

Visual Arts Library/© ADAGP 1988

The Twelve Tribes of Israel: Joseph *1960-62*
133" × 99" Hadassah University Medical Centre, Jerusalem

This commission was of particular emotional significance for Chagall, drawing out his innermost feelings about his Jewish faith. The stained glass was actually executed by the specialist, Charles Marq, based on Chagall's watercolour or gouache models. Chagall then painted the figures on to the surface, adding a personal touch before final firing.

The Twelve Tribes of Israel: Benjamin *1960-62*
133″ × 99″ Hadassah University Medical Centre, Jerusalem

*Working in stained glass gave Chagall's love of rich colours full rein
and gave each of the twelve windows of this series a particular
dominant hue, such as gold for* The Tribe of Joseph *opposite. Here,*
The Tribe of Benjamin *is shown as a beast of prey on a vivid blue
ground below a huge rosette; Jerusalem is shown behind in yellow.*

The Colony of La Ruche

**An exhibition pavilion incongruously re-erected in a poor quarter of
Paris, La Ruche was home to a motley band of talented artists who
were later to become major figures in 20th-century art.**

At the beginning of this century, the Vaugirard
district of Paris, in the 15th *arrondissement*, was a
dirty, impoverished area with miserable living
conditions. The stench of blood, drifting from the
nearby slaughterhouses, hung on the air, and
there was little respite from the daytime bellowing
of the cattle, or the drunken rampages of the *tueurs*
– the killers employed in the abattoirs – who
terrorized the neighbourhood by night.

It was here that the artists of La Ruche
congregated in a curious structure which was
shaped rather like a beehive and surrounded by
tiny, ramshackle studios. La Ruche itself was a
pavilion which had been salvaged from the
Universal Exhibition of 1900 by the sculptor Alfred
Boucher. Boucher re-erected it in the Danzig Alley,
founding a commune, as a magnanimous gesture,

Mary Evans Picture Library

Gilbert Martin Guillou/Explorer

A hive of activity
*(left) A haven for poor
artists and writers from
all over Europe, La Ruche
was an exciting complex
of studios which teemed
with activity.*

**Miserable
surroundings**
*(above) La Ruche was
situated in the Vaugirard
district – a depressing
area dominated by the
slaughterhouses.*

for impoverished artists working in Paris.
Peppercorn rents were charged for the tiny wedge-
shaped studios radiating off the central staircase.
These studios were dubbed 'coffins' by their
inmates, most of whom could barely afford even
the modest rents, and often had to be helped out
by the kindly concierge, Madame Segondet.

A visitor to the commune would be greeted by
piles of rubbish and jettisoned canvases blocking
the dank alleyways, the constant dripping of water
and, as likely as not, the pungent smell of some
rotting still life which a painter had been working
from for weeks in his garret. But to some of the
artists, La Ruche was an Elysium compared to the
situation they had left at home.

Most of them were foreigners, or *métèques* as the
Parisians disparagingly called them: Russians,
Poles, Spaniards, Italians and Germans. La Ruche
became a refuge for Jewish émigrés escaping
persecution by the police and the pogroms –

Brera, Milan

eccentric figure with her leather sandals and her floating Liberty dresses when the *haut monde* of Paris was tripping around in Paul Poiret's hobble-skirts. 'The done thing was to be or at least look abnormal or strange', Vlaminck remembered.

They were all odd. And none more so than Chagall, with his pale face and made-up eyes, painting his dreams of Vitebsk by gaslight at the dead of night, stark naked in front of his canvases. Chagall was the 'millionaire' among them; with his tiny income he could afford one of the larger 'coffins' on the top floor of La Ruche. Soutine, having worked feverishly for hours, and faint with hunger, would sometimes thunder up the central staircase and hammer on Chagall's door, demanding a few crusts of bread. Chagall kept all his visitors waiting, while he put on some clothes and nervously turned all his fresh canvases to the wall to avoid inquisitive, competitive eyes.

SHARED POVERTY

He always found something for his poor compatriot to eat. 'On the shelves', he wrote, 'reproductions of El Greco and Cézanne lay next to the remains of a herring I had cut in two, the head for the first day, the tail for the next, and, thank God, a few crusts of bread . . .' Even the 'millionaire' had to resort to painting on sheets, tablecloths and nightshirts when he could not

Bridgeman Art Library

massacres in the Russian ghettos. Painters like Chaim Soutine and Pinchus Kremègne, who arrived at La Ruche in 1913, had suffered utter misery and near-starvation in the ghettos of Smilovitchi near Minsk. La Ruche at least offered liberty, and the encouraging enthusiasm of other high-minded artists. And there was always the colourful diversion of Montparnasse café life, mitigating the squalor of their daily existence.

Chagall settled at La Ruche in 1912. Over the next few years, the lodgers who came and went included the painters Fernand Léger, Soutine and Kremègne, Michel Ki Koine, Moïse Kisling, Jean Metzinger and Modigliani; the sculptors Jacques Lipchitz, Ossip Zadkine and Alexander Archipenko and the poets Blaise Cendrars and Max Jacob. Other friends, like the critic Apollinaire and even Jean Cocteau would drop in occasionally, and there were plenty of hangers-on. Modigliani's girlfriend, Beatrice Hastings, cut an

The handsome Kisling
(above) Modigliani's portrait shows his Polish friend Moïse Kisling. Popular at La Ruche, artists would gather in his studio to work, drink and discuss art long into the night.

The unsociable Soutine
(right) A Russian Jew, Chaim Soutine was melancholy and taciturn, with uncouth manners. Despite his poverty he would leave good food to rot while he completed his still lifes.

Paulette Jourdain/Edimages

The elegant Italian
(left) Modigliani moved to Montparnasse in 1909, three years after arriving in Paris, and was a frequent visitor at La Ruche, where his friends Kisling and Soutine lived and worked. From a cultured Italian Jewish family, he was usually extremely well dressed, and was an entertaining, extrovert figure.

La Rotonde
(below) In the years before the First World War, the artistic centre shifted from Montmartre to Montparnasse, and local café life took off. La Rotonde was a favourite haunt of artists and students, and Libion, the patron, amassed a fine collection of paintings in return for food and drink.

H. Roger Viollet

afford canvas.

All the artists worked immensely hard, often congregating in Kisling's studio where they would share the cost of a model. Chagall kept aloof, but the others often found it easier to work together, and when the painting session was through, their animated discussions were fuelled by quantities of alcohol and the inevitable hashish pills. Artificial stimulants were an easy escape from the depression of obscurity and poverty.

Occasionally cartloads of canvases would be seen making their way towards the wooden booths near the Place de L'Alma, destined for the Salon exhibitions. But sales were few and far between. A Polish expatriate, Zborowski, took on a handful of the La Ruche artists, including Modigliani, Soutine and Kisling, and tried to promote their work. But he had far less success than the dealers patronizing the avant-garde painters of the Picasso gang – the 'arrogant Cubists' as Chagall called them.

Many of Picasso's followers still lived in Montmartre, but Montparnasse was by now the centre of bohemian café life. La Rotonde, at the crossroads of the Boulevarde Raspail and the Boulevarde Montparnasse, was the most popular café, buzzing with artists and their models, the odd cocotte and a few dope peddlars. In the

H. Veiller/Explorer

corner, a gloomy group with little goatee beards would sit over interminable games of chess. One of them was Trotsky, and occasionally he would be joined by Lunacharsky or Lenin. It was rumoured that the plans for the Russian Revolution were hatched in a backroom at La Rotonde.

Libion, the generous patron, would let the artists sit all day over a single cup of coffee, and he was happy to exchange a ham sandwich or some sauerkraut for their paintings, when there was no cash. In the café, the artists could sketch the clientele in exchange for a few drinks, and, after a few too many, Modigliani in particular was always good for some entertainment. He was fond of quoting passages from Dante, Nostradamus or Oscar Wilde, but when it came to art, discussions of Cubism with Vlaminck or Derain, Braque or Picasso roused him to fury. Chagall ignored them, but Modigliani fought with his fists. Later on in the evening, perhaps at one of Maria Wassilieff's wild parties, he could be relied on to indulge his natural exhibitionism: everyone knew exactly when to expect the clothes to come off.

If he was not abusing the Cubists, Modigliani would be venting his temper on Beatrice Hastings. 'Help! He's killing me!' was the normal cry ringing out from her flat on the rue Montparnasse. Once he bundled her out of the window in exasperation. But friends would also have to dress the vicious bites she gave him by way of retribution.

Chagall disliked these excesses. He did not drink, and did not have the self-destructive streak which characterized many of his fellow lodgers at La Ruche. In 1914, he left for Russia, having wired up his studio door. When he returned after the war, it had been broken into. His easel and many of his paintings had been sold, and there was a new tenant. Things had changed. But the years of obscurity were over. Chagall, Soutine and others

who survived the penury of La Ruche found themselves hailed, with their old rivals in the Picasso gang, as members of the famous School of Paris. Even the flea-ridden, inarticulate Soutine, whom Modigliani had taught to blow his nose with a handkerchief rather than his fingers, developed a taste for the luxury which accompanied success, and was to be seen sporting silk shirts, to the amusement of his friends.

Champion and critic
(left) The poet and art critic Guillaume Apollinaire – depicted here by his mistress, the French painter and designer Marie Laurencin – was a staunch supporter and spokesman for the Cubists and Futurists, and took up the cause of Chagall and other artists of La Ruche. A jovial man whom Chagall called 'that sweet Zeus', Apollinaire was at the centre of the Parisian cultural scene.

Edimages/© ADAGP 1988

Colleagues and friends
(right) Although there was rivalry between the artists of La Ruche and the Picasso gang, they were all later grouped together as 'the School of Paris', and there was some fraternization between the two camps. They also shared mutual friends like Apollinaire and the bald poet and journalist Max Jacob – a sad person who disguised his shyness with flamboyant clothes and a dissolute lifestyle. Jacob is shown here with his close friend Picasso (in cap) on the terrace outside La Rotonde.

Jean-Loup Charmet

A Year in the Life 1941

In 1941, Chagall, like many other artists, sought refuge from Nazi-dominated Europe in the United States. But the European struggle was now turning into a world war. Germany invaded the USSR, and the USA was drawn into the conflict by Japan's devastating attack on Pearl Harbor.

In the early months of 1941, the Axis powers controlled most of Europe, opposed only by Britain and her Dominions. There was alarm for the safety of shipping convoys in May, when the German super-battleship *Bismarck* broke out into the Atlantic. When she was located, her powerful guns destroyed the *Hood* and damaged the *Prince of Wales;* but by then she was crippled by torpedo-planes from the *Ark Royal,* and the other British ships finished her off.

On land, the British seemed to be winning for a time. In both North and East Africa, the numerically superior Italian armies were routed without showing any great will to resist. However, the British advance in Libya was slowed when troops were diverted to Greece, where a new crisis was looming. The Italians had invaded Greece in October 1940, but here too they

Attack on Pearl Harbor
(below) At 7.55am on 7 December, the Japanese launched a massive surprise air attack on Pearl Harbor, America's major outlying naval base located on the Hawaiian island of Oahu. Here a launch is rescuing a survivor from the blazing battleship West Virginia.

Bulloz

Bibliothèque Nationale

Jean-Loup Charmet

Indian poet
(above) The Bengali mystical poet and author, Sir Rabindranath Tagore, died in August 1941, aged 80. His work had earned him the Nobel prize for literature in 1913.

Rommel and his staff
(left) The defeat of their Italian allies in the Western Desert led the German High Command to despatch General Rommel and two Panzer divisions to North Africa in February 1941.

had suffered humiliating defeats. In April, the Germans struck suddenly, mounting their own invasion and simultaneously attacking Yugoslavia. Their *Blitzkrieg* overran the two countries in a matter of days; the British army was flung back and had to be lifted off by the navy. Then in May, the Germans captured Crete after spectacular though costly airborne landings. The German breakthrough into the Mediterranean was all the more serious because the arrival of General Rommel and two Panzer divisions had transformed the situation in North Africa, where the Germans reached the Egyptian frontier by mid-April.

Hitler took his greatest gamble on 22 June. At 3 o'clock in the morning, 3,500,000 Axis troops poured into Soviet Russia in a devastating surprise attack. Smolensk and Kiev fell, Leningrad was surrounded, and the German armies pressed on towards Moscow. But winter approached, and the advance began to slow down as Stalin's 'scorched earth' policy and the vast distances took their toll of the German war machine. Early in December, 'General Winter' stopped the invader in his tracks.

The invasion of the USSR took some of the pressure off Britain, since the Luftwaffe was now needed in the East. Winston Churchill immediately concluded an alliance with Stalin, and British factories began producing war materials for the Russians. The United States Congress passed the Lend Lease Act extending huge credits which did not have to be repaid until after the war. In August, Churchill and President Roosevelt met on ship and issued an 'Atlantic Charter' affirming democratic values. But the USA did not enter the war until the Japanese, on December 7, launched a surprise carrier-

'Operation Barbarossa' *(right and below) The German-Soviet non-aggression pact of 1939 had kept the USSR out of the war as supplier of materials in return for German acknowledgement of Russian territorial interests in Eastern Europe. Hitler, however, had long declared his eventual aim of conquering Russia, exterminating the Slavs and expanding eastwards. The German surprise invasion of Russian territory on 22 June was portrayed by Nazi propaganda as a conflict of ideology – Communism versus Fascism – as seen in this French poster. The German advance was fast and vicious, gambling on a speedy victory. But they had not bargained for the tenacity of the Russian people.*

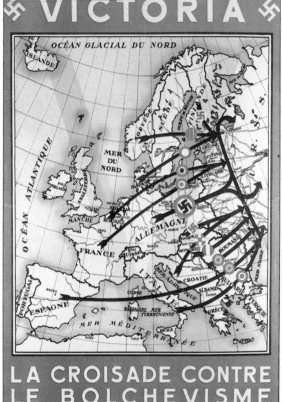

Musée de la Resistance, Paris

Jean-Loup Charmet

Archiv für Kunst und Geschichte

Archiv für Kunst und Geschichte

borne air attack that crippled the US Pacific Fleet based on Pearl Harbor in Hawaii. When Japan's allies, Germany and Italy, declared war on the USA, the conflict became truly world-wide.

At the year's end, Rommel was in retreat and the Russians were counter-attacking. But in the East, the Japanese were triumphant over a huge area of South-East Asia and the Pacific, and seemed poised to strike at British India and Australia.

RUDOLF HESS PAYS A VISIT

The most bizarre incident of 1941 was the arrival via parachute of Deputy Führer Rudolf Hess in Scotland. He believed he could negotiate an Anglo-German peace with the King. This was also the year when clothes rationing was introduced in Britain, and standardized basic ('Utility') clothes and furniture came on the market. Income tax was raised to 10/- (50 per cent) in the pound. Bombs destroyed the House of Commons. Communists organized a 'People's Convention' against the war, and their newspaper, the *Daily Worker*, was suppressed; after Hitler's invasion of Russia, they became ardent supporters of the anti-Fascist struggle.

Orson Welles's film *Citizen Kane* appeared in 1941 and a number of figures, eminent in the seemingly remote pre-war period, died: Baden-Powell, founder of the Boy Scout movement; Kaiser Wilhelm II, German emperor during the First World War; the flier Amy Johnson; the two great modern writers, James Joyce and Virginia Woolf; and Paderewski, pianist and sometime prime minister of Poland.

Citizen Kane
(below) RKO Pictures released Orson Welles' film masterpiece in 1941, despite a threatened law suit from press baron William Randolph Hearst. The film, loosely based on the true life stories of Hearst and Howard Hughes, brilliantly traced the rise to fame and empty power of a fictitious newspaper magnate.

The Four Year Plan
(above) This Nazi propaganda poster of 1941 is a celebration and reminder of the Four Year Plan initiated by Hitler in 1936 and entrusted to leading Nazi, Hermann Goering. Hitler's masterplan for a new world order required an economy geared to the manufacture of armaments and industrial self-sufficiency.

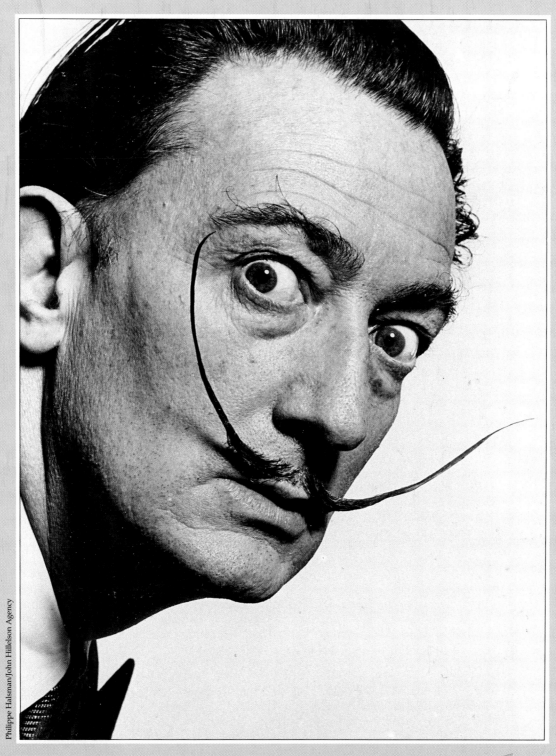

SALVADOR DALÍ

b.1904

One of the most universally famous artists of the 20th century, Salvador Dalí has had a significant influence on art ever since his emergence within the Surrealist movement in 1929. His development of Surrealist theory led him to simulate a form of 'reasoning madness' which made him hypersensitive to the hidden meaning behind an innocent image. He used this 'paranoiac-critical method' in some of his most successful paintings.

Despite being so strongly identified with Surrealism, Dalí has dissociated himself from the movement since 1938 and has turned to Classicism, describing this change of direction as 'a religious Renaissance based on a progressive Catholicism'. Equally fluent in words as in painting, Dalí's pronouncements have contributed much to his popular image as a personality – as well as an artist – of considerable controversy.

A Great Showman

While Dalí often behaved outrageously, he was serious and singleminded about his art. His wife Gala, whom he met at the beginning of his Surrealist phase, remained a constant inspiration.

Key Dates

1904 born in Figueras, Spain

1921 enters the School of Fine Arts, Madrid

1925 first exhibition in Barcelona

1926 visits Paris. Expelled from the University

1929 officially joins the Paris Surrealists

1930 buys cottage at Port Lligat

1936 represented in the International Surrealist Exhibition, London

1938 visits Freud in London

1940 with the fall of France, goes to America. Breaks with the Surrealists

1964 awarded the highest decoration in Spain, Grand Cross of Isabella the Catholic.

1978 elected to the Beaux-Arts Academy

1983 fire at his home when Dalí at 80 is severely burnt

Salvador Dalí was born on 11 May 1904, in the provincial Catalan town of Figueras in Spain. His father was a prominent notary with strong Republican views. He adored his mother, who was a pious Catholic. The name Salvador had been given to his brother who had died nine months before his own birth, and his parents, compensating for their grief, thoroughly spoilt their new son. Nonetheless, Dalí felt a substitute and in his autobiography gives a vivid account of his morbid self-identification with his dead brother and his desire for attention.

EARLY ARTISTIC TALENT

Dalí showed an early interest in art, producing his first painting in 1910, when he was only six. Although his father showed no opposition to his son's aptitude, he did insist that he obtained his baccalaureate and pursue an official academic career. After two unsuccessful attempts to educate the young Salvador at the local schools, his bizarre behaviour and his refusal to learn anything suggested to his teachers that they were dealing with an extraordinary but abnormal personality. Everything strange or phenomenal that happened during his early schooling was attributed to him. 'He is really mad', they would say. And Dalí savoured that phrase ever after. Later he was to say, 'At the age of six I wanted to be a cook. At seven I wanted to be Napoleon. And my ambition has been growing ever since'.

In September 1921, his father allowed him to enter the School of Fine Arts in Madrid. He had by this time produced a number of paintings, had

Archiv für Kunst und Geschichte/© DACS 1988

won two prizes and was full of confidence.

Settling in at the University, Dalí devoted himself to studying, sketching at the Prado and perfecting his technique. He met Lorca, the great Spanish poet, and Luis Buñuel, with whom he later collaborated on the two most remarkable Surrealist films ever made, *Un Chien Andalou* and *L'Age d'or*. During this period Dalí felt himself to be far in advance of most of the other students. He was familiar with the new art movements that were coming out of Paris through such reviews as *L'Esprit Nouveau* and the Italian *Valori Plastici,* in which he discovered the Cubist works of Picasso and the paintings of Giorgio de Chirico. The latter's strange deserted Italian squares, arcades and towers were to have a great influence on his early Surrealist work. One of his most important discoveries was Freud's *Interpretation of Dreams*, which explores the unconscious. Every event, however accidental, Dalí subjected to self-interpretation. Through the theories of Freud he could prove that his wildest dreams and nightmares made sense.

It was not long before Dalí became dissatisfied with the teaching ability of the Academy. 'I

Dalí's birthplace
Figueras is in Catalonia which has a strong separatist movement and Republican tradition against which Dalí reacted by becoming a Monarchist. His birthplace now houses the Dalí museum.

FiroFoto

Summer days
(left) Dalí's family had a house by the sea at Cadaqués where the artist spent his holidays. This beach lies in front of the house and one of the family's two boats is pulled up awaiting the afternoon ride. The group in the foreground features the family returning from Mass and includes Dalí's sister, Ana-Maria, who remembers posing for the picture.

The artist's father
(below) Dalí's father was a dominating character, an atheist and a Republican. Although he never discouraged Dalí's talent, he wanted his son to have a conventional education leading to a secure academic career. But Dalí reacted strongly against his father both in his career and politically.

Museo Perrot-Moore, Cadaques

expected to find limits, rigour, science. I was offered liberty, laziness, approximations', he said. In 1923, for an act of insubordination he was suspended for a year. Returning to his parents' summer house in Cadaqués, he decided it was to be a time of discipline, giving himself over 'body and soul' to painting.

At the end of the year he was back in Madrid, fully prepared to continue his previous life-style. He bought the most expensive suits, silk shirts, sapphire cufflinks, charging them all to his father. With his old friends he haunted the cafés of the city, joining in artistic and literary discussions. His reputation for irreverence and rebellion brought him before the disciplinary committee of the University and he was permanently expelled.

EXPERIMENTS WITH STYLE

During the years which followed, Dalí was to go through several opposing experiments. He explored the idea of capturing movement in painting after seeing the work of the Italian Futurists and then turned his enquiring mind to the enigmatic and disquieting dream imagery of Chirico. He even tried his hand at painting in the style of Vermeer, while still continuing with the abstract subject-matter of Cubism.

In 1925, when Picasso was visiting Barcelona, he had seen one of Dalí's paintings of which he had spoken highly; it was at Dalí's first one-man show at the Dalmau Gallery in Barcelona. A year

AISA © DACS 1988

Museum of Modern Art, Barcelona

Edimedia

The new Surrealist
The photograph shows Dalí at the age of 25 when he officially joined the Surrealists. His neat appearance contrasts sharply with the long hair and bohemian dress of his student days.

The Surrealists

In 1924, the first Surrealist manifesto was published in Paris and the Surrealist movement came into being. As an alternative to 'the rule of logic', the Surrealists began to explore the depths of the mind, in particular the unconscious. Heavily influenced by Freud, they saw in dreams and free association a means by which they could discover a new reality. Poets and painters were encouraged to research into every field, and reconcile what had previously been irreconcilable.

Archiv für Kunst und Geschichte

André Breton
(left) This French poet was the founder of the Surrealist movement. He was anti-rational, believing that the exploration of the unconscious would reveal new truths.

The Surrealist Revolution
(right) Many well-known people contributed to this first issue of the Surrealist periodical – poets like Paul Eluard, and painters like Max Ernst, and even Picasso who was not a Surrealist.

Jean-Loup Charmet

later, Dalí decided to make a brief visit to Paris to see Picasso. Full of respect, he said, 'I have come to see you before visiting the Louvre'. 'You are quite right,' Picasso is reported to have replied.

Inspired by Picasso, he returned home to produce a number of large Cubist canvases, but the discipline this required acted as a restraint. He was possessed by an overwhelming desire to ally his subjective visions with painting, to give his work 'the real processes of thought'. Surrealism pointed the way.

When Dalí returned to Paris in 1929, it was not to see Picasso, but his friend Miró. 'Have you a dinner suit?' Miró asked him. Dalí bought one the next day, and so began his entrée into Paris society. He dined with the rich and famous. The social round was endless and Dalí was quick to appreciate the advantages. 'That I had reached fame, I felt and knew the moment I landed at the Gare d'Orsay in Paris . . . I began to look around me, and from then on I regarded most of the people I met solely and exclusively as creatures I could use as posters in my voyages of ambition.'

A.G.E. Fotostock

AUTOMATIC PAINTING

He met the Surrealists and their founder, André Breton, attended their discussions and read their Manifestos. When Camille Goemans offered him a Paris exhibition, he went back to Spain to put his work together. Back in Cadaqués, his immediate thought was to capture the strange images that were taking possession of his mind. He felt

the touch of madness. This time his paintings would be completely automatic without any conscious intervention and he would reproduce this stream of mental activity with absolute clarity and as scrupulously as possible.

Among the many visitors to Cadaqués during this period was the Surrealist poet, Paul Eluard, and his wife Gala. They were distressed at Dalí's general mental state – his convulsions and bursts

Source of inspiration
The rocky coastline of Catalonia often recurs as a setting for Dalí's paintings. He and his wife, Gala, made their home at Port Lligat, a fishing village, overlooking the sea.

of hysterical laughter. It was suggested that Gala might speak to him. This meeting was the beginning of their great love and she remained behind when her husband left.

When his new works arrived in Paris, there was little doubt where his sympathies lay. André Breton wrote in the foreword to the catalogue, 'It is perhaps with Dalí that all the great mental windows are opening'. He left no doubt of the importance Dalí brought to Surrealism; at the same time he also voiced certain reservations. He saw him as a man poised between talent and genius – but also, perhaps, between vice and virtue. The systematized imagery that Dalí was now entering into had its origin in psychoanalysis, in the case histories of Freud and Krafft-Ebing. For the first time in Surrealism he sought to use both the automatism that had dominated Surrealism since the 1920s and the dream narrative.

DALÍ THE WRITER

In true Renaissance tradition, Dalí set out to involve himself in every aspect of creative thought. Apart from poems and essays he, on average, produced a book every two years. The most revealing is *The Secret Life of Salvador Dalí*, the book which George Orwell described as 'a striptease act conducted in pink limelight'.

With his ceaseless invention, Dalí soon achieved a position of considerable importance in the Surrealist movement. He rediscovered 'art nouveau', whose architecture he considered 'the most original and extraordinary phenomenon in the history of art'. Many of the ectoplasmic forms in his works of this period are drawn from the ornamentation on the Paris subways and the Gaudí architecture in Barcelona. He also evolved what he called the 'paranoiac-critical method' of

Luis Buñuel
(above) The great Spanish film director Buñuel (right in the photograph) and Dalí collaborated to produce the Surrealist film Un Chien Andalou *in 1928. It showed a series of extraordinary, inexplicable images – like a hand covered in crawling ants – which Buñuel claimed symbolized nothing. The next year they planned* L'Age d'or, *but by this time they had grown apart and it was much more Buñuel's film than Dalí's, despite the use of many images from Dalí's paintings.*

FiroFoto

Philippe Halsman/John Hillelson Agency

Photographic portraits
Dalí worked with Philippe Halsman on a series of photographs of himself. This one is called 'Atomicus' because, as in the atom, each ingredient of the photograph is suspended in space.

Daniel Farson/BBC Hulton Picture Library

contribute to exhibitions that were taking place. On the occasion of the International Surrealist Exhibition in London in 1936, Dalí gave a lecture in a diving suit while holding two Russian wolfhounds on a lead. He was not only inaudible, but nearly suffocated before someone could remove the helmet.

Dalí met Edward James, the millionaire, who became his patron and bought many of his most important works. Two years later he achieved his greatest ambition, to see Sigmund Freud who had settled in London after his escape from Hitler's Germany. After Dalí left, Freud said to a friend, 'I have never seen a more complete example of a Spaniard. What a fanatic!'

Between 1937 and 1939, Dalí began to react against his early work. He announced a return to

The Influence of Freud

Sigmund Freud is the accepted founder of psychoanalysis. He had discovered that one of his patients, under hypnosis, could recall emotional experiences hitherto forgotten, and that the recall seemed to alleviate the symptoms of mental disturbance. Freud's great contribution therefore was to stress the value of memories and experiences buried in the unconscious, and the importance of dreams and free association as ways of reaching them. The Surrealists were interested in the liberation of the imagination this implied, and Dalí, with his own intense and complex imagination, was lastingly influenced by Freud.

Mary Evans/Sigmund Freud Copyrights/W.E. Freud

Gala
Dalí was absolutely devoted to his wife Gala and she was a constant inspiration to him as his many paintings of her testify. Because she was married when Dalí met her, his father banished Dalí from the Figueras house for several years. But Gala's advent was immensely important to Dalí as she allayed the sexual anxieties which were driving him to the edge of madness.

looking at art, in which he recognized hidden meanings in such works as Millet's painting *The Angelus*, and also in the legend of William Tell.

It was Dalí's proposal that the catalogue for the Surrealist exhibition should include a eulogy of Meissonier. This was no doubt inspired by his love of academic classical painting, but also by a certain perversity. He also resolved to stay aloof from the political stand that the Surrealists were taking against the rise of Fascism, while at the same time he portrayed Lenin in an uncomplimentary manner in a painting and showed a swastika on the armband of a nurse sitting in a pool of water in another work. Outraged, Breton called a meeting of the Surrealists and listed the charges against Dalí. Surrealism was not prepared to sponsor Dalí's private obsessions. However, not all the members agreed and the affair petered out. Thereafter, Dalí ceased to attend any of the official meetings, although he was still invited to classicism, to the pictorial science of the Renaissance. From now on it was to be not experimentation, but tradition.

Dalí had made his first visit to New York in 1934 and called it his 'American Campaign'. He was to continue it when, with the advent of war, he arrived in New York with his wife Gala.

THE TALK OF NEW YORK

The sensational publicity of the Surrealists in Paris had already reached the States and Dalí's appeal was immediate. His flair for showmanship soon made him the talk of New York, which he described as 'an immense Gothic Roquefort Cheese'. Soon he was undertaking commissions for window displays, lectures and film scenarios.

Private Collection

The father of psychoanalysis
(left) Dalí read Freud's Interpretation of Dreams *as a student, and said it was 'one of the capital discoveries of my life . . . I was seized with a real vice of self-interpretation, not only of my dreams but of everything that happened to me . . .'*

Dismal Sport (1929)
(above) This marked Dalí's debut as a Surrealist. He worked at the painting with feverish intensity during the summer at Cadaqués, and many of his obsessions surface in it, such as his childhood horror of grasshoppers, and his traumatic sexual fears.

A. G. F. Fotostock/© DACS 1988

Museo Dalí, Figueras

He created the dream sequence in Hitchcock's *Spellbound* and had an entire orchestra floating out to sea on a raft in one of the Marx Brothers' films.

With the advent of the war, many of the Surrealists who had so vigorously opposed Nazism succeeded in reaching America, where they soon established their presence. They were quick to resume their attacks on Dalí. Breton even coined an anagram of his name 'Avida Dollars' (greedy dollars) as a form of protest against the artist's money-making antics.

Still passing himself off as the only authentic Surrealist, Dalí continued to strengthen his belief in a Catholic hierarchy and the monarchy, going as far as to seek the approval of the Pope for one of his paintings. He began speaking of himself as 'The Cosmic Dalí'. Writing in 1958, he said, 'It is difficult to hold the world's interest for more than half an hour at a time. I myself have done so successfully every day for twenty years.'

The Face of Mae West
Dalí designed this room to look like the face of Mae West. It has been created in the Dalí museum with her blonde hair transformed into curtains framing the room as though it were a stage. Her nose has become a fireplace with pictures either side doubling as eyes. Perhaps the most famous object in the room is the sofa in the shape of Mae West's lips. Dalí enjoyed designing things whose appearance belied their true purpose and function.

Surrealism and Classicism

An exceptional pictorial skill and an imaginative extremism made Dalí the ideal interpreter and popularizer of Surrealism. He has since successfully married these gifts to a renewed interest in tradition.

Perls Galleries, N.Y.

When Dalí joined the Surrealist movement in 1929, he was to turn Surrealist research in a particular direction, which previously had only been approached in a tentative fashion, and carry it to its extreme conclusion. He declared that his art evolved from a constant, hallucinatory energy and proposed that he would paint like a madman rather than a somnambulist recording his dreams.

The first theoretical foundations of the movement were laid in 1924 under the direction of André Breton. Then Surrealism dedicated itself to the unconscious as the essential source of all art in order to bring about a complete revision of values. In the *First Surrealist Manifesto*, Breton describes Surrealism as 'pure psychic automatism, by which it is intended to express, verbally, in writing or by other means, the real process of thought; thought's dictation, in the absence of all control exercised by reason, and outside all aesthetic or moral preoccupation'. It was therefore clearly defined as purely intuitive. Only in automatic writing, in fantasies and dreams, could the stream of consciousness manifest itself.

At this time it was held that no such thing as Surrealist painting could exist since painting was too conscious an act. But by 1925, Breton did not see the definition in quite that way and believed that art could be an instrument of discovery. The inherent weakness of automatism did not, however, escape the Surrealists, who saw in their

The Architectonic Angelus of Millet (1933)
(above) Millet's Angelus, which shows a man and woman in prayer, obsessed Dalí for some years. He saw the woman as a type of sexual predator, and in one painting on the subject depicts the man with a death's head. Here, the two figures are reduced to prehistoric monuments.

The Phantom Chariot (c.1933)
(right) Dalí's realistic technique is a witty tool for overturning reality. Here the figures in the cart can be read as part of the townscape – but which view is the true one, and which an illusion?

Private Collection

The Madonna of Port Lligat (1949)
(above) The atomic explosion at Hiroshima in 1945 profoundly affected Dalí. Here, the potent idea of the divisibility of matter is linked to an Italian Renaissance masterpiece – Piero della Francesca's Brera altarpiece. Gala is the model for the Madonna, and she is mysteriously suspended above the bay of Dalí's own fishing village. Despite the painting's fragmented structures, the prevailing sense is of powerful forces perfectly juxtaposed and balanced.

work the danger of repetition and monotony in the absence of any conscious control.

Dalí, while fully in accord with the Surrealists' use of a form of free expression inspired by dreams, saw that the full potential of the strange and often violent imagery that came into his mind could only be developed in a fully conscious manner. This did not mean that he censored the free association of what he saw, but that he gave it a concrete reality by applying to it his considerable artistic skill. He was, he declared, painting 'handmade photography'. By the use of a photo-realist technique, he captured and recorded the images he saw.

THE PARANOIAC-CRITICAL METHOD

His deep and lasting preoccupation with the writings of Freud and with psychoanalysis led him to develop what he called the 'paranoiac-critical method'. In simple terms this is a form of image interpretation depending on the imaginative

ability of the onlooker, and not unlike the lesson taught by Leonardo da Vinci, that one should study the stains upon a wall in which might be seen strange monsters. In this way the eye can discover another world, which painting then makes concrete.

During 1937 and 1938, Dalí produced a number of paintings in which he explored the use of multiple simultaneous images. They came about as a result of his ability to simulate the disordered mind of the paranoiac and to perceive the image behind an appearance, without becoming mentally disturbed himself. He stated this most pertinently when he said, 'The only difference between myself and a madman is that I am not mad'. A clear example of this practice is the *Metamorphosis of Narcissus* (pp.122-3), in which a fossil-like hand holds an egg from which sprouts a narcissus flower. This is transformed into the image of the youth Narcissus, who, in Greek mythology, fell in love with his own reflection.

Simultaneously with his development of multiple images, Dalí turned his attention to Millet's devout picture *The Angelus*, where the man

The Ghost of Vermeer of Delft, Which Can Be Used As a Table (1934) *(below) This painting draws together several of Dalí's obsessions – with the Dutch painter Vermeer, and with food and furniture. Originally, he wanted to paint a ghost serving as a chair, but the idea of using Vermeer's thigh as a table, with a bottle and a glass of wine perched on it, was so magnificently illogical that he could not resist it. Dalí's intense dislike of all things mechanical often led him to devise and surround himself with furniture that takes on a human shape (see* The Face of Mae West *p.113).*

COMPARISONS

Precursors of Surrealism

The founder of Surrealism, André Breton, stated that 'Surrealism existed before me, and I firmly believe that it will survive me'. It was a belief shared by all the Surrealists, and they set about promoting artists of the past whose work had traditionally been neglected or misunderstood, and whom they considered to be forerunners of their movement. The most important visionary painter to them was Hieronymus Bosch, and Dalí himself also greatly admired the Italian Renaissance masters, especially Leonardo da Vinci.

Reproduced by gracious permission of Her Majesty the Queen

Detail: Royal Library, Windsor

Archiv für Kunst und Geschichte

Prado. Madrid

Hieronymus Bosch (c.1450-1516) The Garden of Earthly Delights
(detail left) The weirdness of Bosch's vision revealed realms of the imagination that the Surrealists were intent on exploring as a means of undermining the repression of reason.

Leonardo da Vinci (1452-1519) Study for the Trivulzio Equestrian Monument
(above) The horse drawings of Leonardo were a direct influence on Dalí, as was his practice of gazing at clouds, water or old surfaces, and discerning fantastic images in them.

and woman are bowed in prayer. Instead of a pious subject, he saw a monstrous image of disguised repression – a complete reversal of what the painting set out to portray. He was to paint many pictures on his interpretation, and in some Leonardo's *Mona Lisa* and Freud's study of that picture also feature. Breton and the Surrealists had earlier expressed some doubts about the direction Dalí's work was now taking. From the Surrealist point of view, he was using his method to produce some undeniably important paintings, but without any attempt to resolve the principal problems of life. By 1933, Breton had attacked Dalí for his political opinions and for the monotony and repetition of his paintings, and went on to state 'that the refinement of the paranoiac-critical method had reduced Dalí to concocting entertainment on the level of crossword puzzles'.

REDISCOVERING THE CLASSICAL

Dalí made a number of visits to Italy between 1937 and 1939. Here he began to strengthen his ties with the Italian tradition and developed a renewed esteem for such artists as Botticelli, Raphael, Uccello and Velázquez, who were now added to his earlier idols, Vermeer and Leonardo. Their

influence became noticeable in the new freedom and bold handling in paintings such as *Palladio's Corridor of Thalia, Impressions of Africa* and many others. Unlike his earlier works, his compositions were now rigidly based on a classical formula, reflecting a more conscious art. No doubt he remembered what Freud had said to him: 'In classical paintings, I look for the unconscious; in a Surrealist painting, for the conscious'. Dalí was now seeing it as a pronouncement of death on Surrealism as a doctrine.

For all his commitment to the Old Masters, Dalí continued his restless search for new ideas and pictorial experiments. His works of this later period show a bewildering mixture of Pop Art, Abstract Expressionism and science. The explosion of the atom bomb in 1945 was to inspire a number of paintings, of which *The Madonna of Port Lligat* is the most representative.

Between 1929 and 1939, the bizarre and revelatory nature of Dalí's imagery was the most potent of our age. He himself pronounced the end of this influential period when he said, 'The two worst things that can happen to an ex-Surrealist today are firstly to become a mystic, and secondly to know how to draw. Both these forms of vigour have lately befallen me at one and the same time'.

Spain

In this painting, dated 1938, Dalí uses the figure of a woman to symbolize the Spanish Civil War. He viewed the War 'as a phenomenon of natural history as opposed to Picasso who considered it a political phenomenon'. He saw this confrontation of elemental forces as being, paradoxically, necessary to reveal the indestructible bones of a tradition that 'this earth of Spain held hidden in the depths of its entrails'. Here Dalí paints the woman's head and upper part of her body in such a way that they can be read as groups of Renaissance warriors locked in battle. These are based on Leonardo's drawings of fighting horsemen. Dalí painted other works at this time using the same device of double imagery, and he exhibited most of them in a one-man show he held in 1939 in the Paris studio he shared with Gala. The first visitor to arrive and the last to leave was Picasso, who particularly wanted to see *Spain*.

'The difference between the Surrealists and me is that I am a Surrealist.'

Salvador Dalí

© DACS 1988

Museum Boymans-van Beuningen Rotterdam

© DACS 1988

Detail: Spain

Double Imagery

An intriguing use of double imagery occurs in many of Dalí's paintings of the 1930s. Thus, for example, the woman's head (detail left) can be seen either as a face with large eyes and a red mouth, or as a man on a plunging horse, and running, struggling figures, one of whom has a red banner or scarf. This shows the technique at its most successful, and it was seen as applicable to other forms of Surrealist activity.

Gallery

Dalí himself referred to his paintings as 'hand-painted dream photographs' and the power of his most characteristic works depends on his ability to invest irrational images with a compelling sense of presence and actuality – in his own words 'to materialize images of concrete irrationality with the most imperialist fury of precision'.

Girl Seated Seen From the Rear
1925
40½" × 29" Museo Español de Arte Contemporaneo, Madrid

This painting was among those shown at Dalí's first one-man exhibition at the Dalmau Gallery in Barcelona in 1925. Picasso saw the exhibition and particularly admired this work. Its enigmatic quality hints at some of Dalí's later preoccupations, but the thick brushwork is strikingly different from the meticulous technique characteristic of his mature work. The model was Dalí's sister.

Pictures such as The Persistence of Memory, The Metamorphosis of Narcissus and The Temptation of St Anthony are conceived with such imaginative brilliance and executed with such finesse that they rank among the most unforgettable works of 20th-century art. Pictorial paradox has rarely reached such heights of sophistication.

For all the clownishness of his public image, Dalí has, since the Second World War, devoted much of his efforts to serious-minded religious paintings. The most famous is undoubtedly Christ of St John of the Cross, which initially caused great controversy but has now attained the status almost of a 20th-century icon.

Woman at the Window at Figueras *c.1926*
9½″ × 10″ Juan Casanelles Collection, Barcelona

Figueras is the town in which Dalí was born and all his life he has retained great affection for his native region. The nearby fishing villages of Cadaqués and Port Lligat as well as Figueras itself feature frequently in his work. Dalí experimented with various styles at this early stage of his career, and here he uses simplified, bulbous forms.

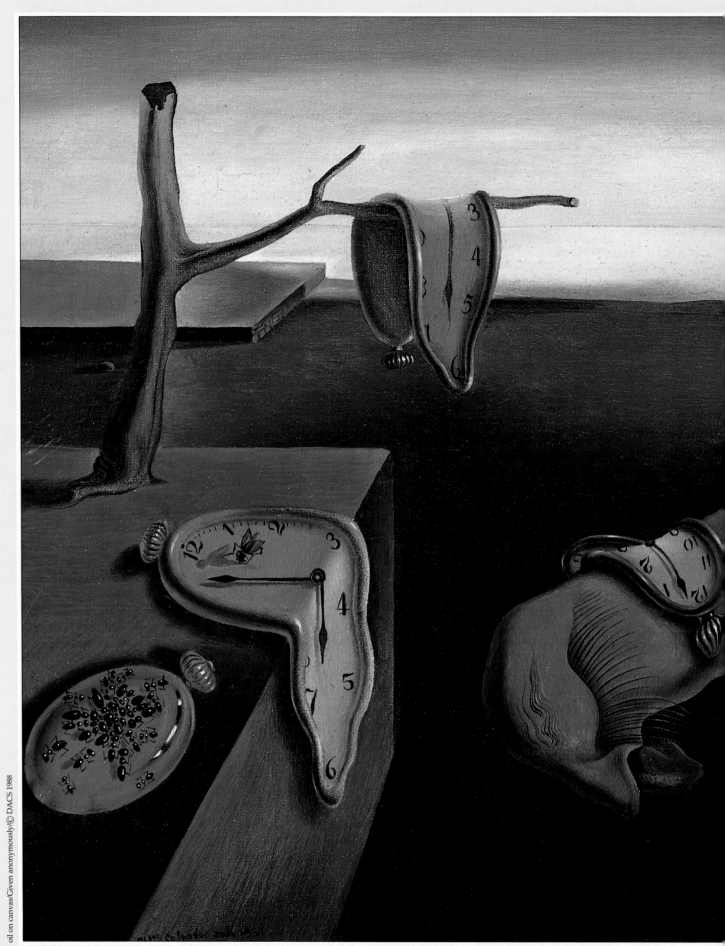

The Persistence of Memory *1931*
9½″ × 13″ Collection, The Museum of
Modern Art, New York

*This is probably the best-known of all Dalí's paintings
and the melting watches have become one of the most
famous and parodied images in 20th-century art. Dalí
himself has commented on his obsession with softness
and he said he had the idea for the watches when he was
eating a ripe camembert cheese. In 1935 he wrote that
'the famous soft clocks are merely the soft, crazy, lonely
paranoiac-critical Camembert of time and space', but the
picture has brought forth many interpretations – the
limp watches, for example, have been seen as indicating
a fear of impotence.*

The Metamorphosis of Narcissus *1937*
20″ × 30¾″ Tate Gallery, London

One of Dalí's most mesmerisingly intense paintings, this picture holds a place among the classic works of Surrealism. In Greek mythology Narcissus was a beautiful youth who fell in love with his own reflection and pined away and died. He was then changed into a flower – the narcissus – by the gods. With its elements of love, death and metamorphosis, the theme held great appeal for a Surrealist artist, and as well as painting the picture, Dalí published a book of the same title.

The Temptation of St Anthony *1946*
35¼″ × 47″ Musées Royaux des
Beaux-Arts, Brussels

Dalí painted this picture for a competition organized by Albert Lewin, an American movie producer who needed a picture of The Temptation of St Anthony for a film on which he was working. Eleven painters entered the competition, which was won by Max Ernst. Ernst's picture was in the late medieval tradition of representations of the subject, featuring hideous demons, but Dalí created a novel symbolic world. St Anthony holds up a cross to ward off evil spirits, which here are manifested as a horse (symbol of aggressive sensuality) and elephants bearing various symbolic devices. On the back of the first, for example, a woman squeezing her breasts and representing lust emerges from a chalice.

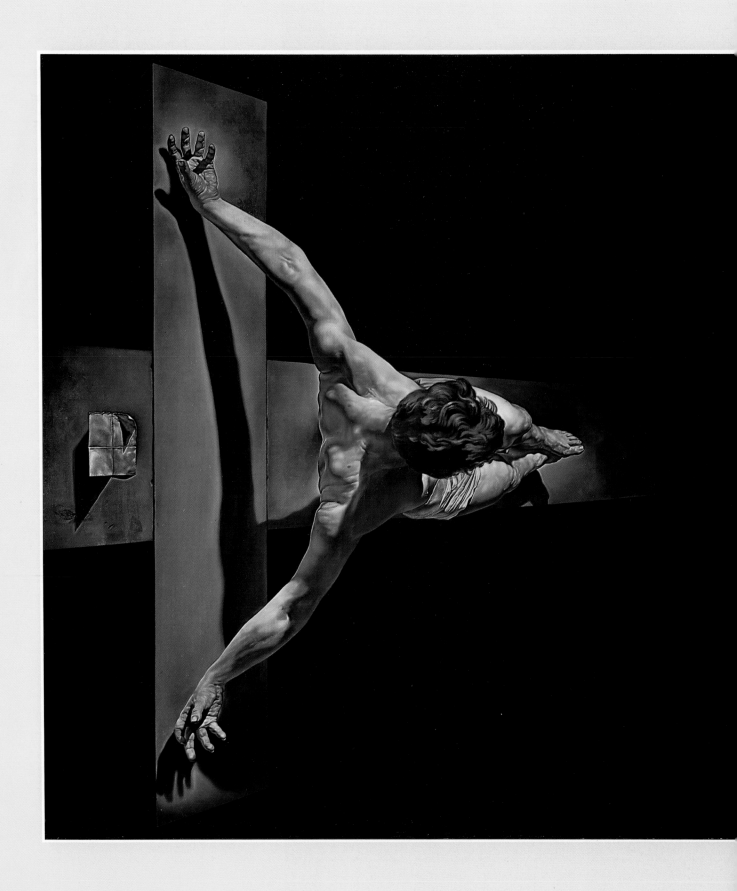

Christ of St John of the Cross 1951
80¾" × 45½" Glasgow Art Gallery and Museum

When this painting was acquired by Glasgow Art Gallery in 1952 for the 'mad price' of £8,200 it became the centre of a storm of controversy because of its alleged sensationalism and was sneered at by critics. Since then it has become enormously popular and has been endlessly reproduced in a multiplicity of contexts throughout the world. The unusual angle from which Christ is seen was inspired by a drawing (now in the Convent of the Incarnation at Avila in Spain) attributed to the 16th century Spanish mystic St John of the Cross.

127

Artothek/© DACS 1988

The Apotheosis of Homer *1945*
25¾″ × 46″ Staatsgalerie Moderner Kunst, Munich

*Here a number of images appear that are familiar from earlier works –
such as the crutch, statue and ants – but this painting was of particular
importance to Dalí in that it represented the end of the Surrealist phase
of his career. In it, Dalí said he wished to give a 'detailed narration of
the world of the blind', and he therefore chose to relate it to Homer, the
greatest poet of antiquity, who was blind.*

Animated Still Life *1956*
49½″ × 63″ The Salvador Dalí Museum,
St Petersburg, Florida

Dalí here wittily overturns the central notion of still life painting – that the objects depicted are inanimate. He perhaps derived the idea from the well-known and brilliant trick photograph of him in his studio (p.111), the similarity in the treatment of the water being particularly striking. Dalí may also have been influenced by the Belgian Surrealist painter René Magritte, but whereas in Magritte's pictures inanimate objects are typically shown hovering statically, Dalí depicts them in vigorous movement.

Barcelona's Revival

Fiercely independent, the Barcelona of Dalí's youth was a forum for artists, writers and musicians from all over the world, a centre which saw a startling blending of tradition and the avant-garde.

Dalí happened to be most closely associated with Barcelona at a particularly exciting moment in its history. The architect Gaudí, the artists Picasso and Miró, and the composers De Falla and Casals were all active in the city during his lifetime. It was here that Dalí found a sufficiently large number of people sympathetic towards avant-garde art to give him his first successes, and an art dealer, Dalmau, who was daring enough to stage Dalí's first one-man show when he was only 21.

As the capital of Catalonia, Barcelona always perceived itself to be fundamentally different from, and rather superior to, other Spanish cities. Although under the political control of Madrid, by the end of the 19th century the city was more economically advanced and 'modern' in its outlook than the Spanish capital. Its industrial strength meant that there was a large population with money to spend on education and entertainment. Cultural tastes were quite wide-ranging and surprisingly

Political paintings
(right) Ramon Casas was a leading figure in the modernista *movement in Catalan painting and a founder of the café* Els Quatre Gats. *The* Garrotting *depicts the fate of eight anarchists who were executed in Barcelona in 1893.*

Architectural extravagance
(below) Combining an exotic variety of architectural styles, the Palau de la Música Catalana was built in 1908.

Museum of Modern Art, Barcelona

The young Picasso
(above) Picasso was 20 years old when Casas made this charcoal, pastel and watercolour portrait of him in 1901. By this time Picasso had already begun to create an impact in Barcelona with the paintings that were to mark the beginning of his 'Blue Period'.

cosmopolitan. Barcelona's rich middle classes flocked to the opera houses to hear performances of Wagner's works, and filled the city's theatres which put on plays by avant-garde European writers like Ibsen, as well as works in Catalan by local playwrights. They enjoyed the mime performances, puppet shows and flamenco dances put on by the music halls, and were happy to buy the constant stream of art objects and artistic furniture that was pouring out from the city's workshops to furnish their new apartments.

A CULTURAL CAPITAL

As Catalonia's fierce desire for political autonomy from Madrid was persistently frustrated, Barcelona's inhabitants had to find other ways of expressing their sense of cultural identity. The first obvious event that encapsulated the city's growing pride was the International Exhibition that took place in 1888. This was designed to present Barcelona to the world as a prosperous, independent and forward-looking city. Its optimistic mood was reflected in the ambitious building programme that was part of the fair, which included the erection of a triumphal arch (the Arc de Triomf), a fan-shaped Palace of Industry, and a Grand Hotel to accommodate visitors to the exhibition which was completed in just 83 days.

The exhibition heralded a boom in construction that changed the very face of Barcelona. As more and more immigrant workers flooded into the city to man the factories, what had once been a medieval walled town burst its confines and stretched out to embrace several neighbouring villages, forming one vast agglomeration. The spate of building that followed gave rise to fervent

Museum of Contemporary Art, Madrid

The Parc Guell
(below) Even park benches were transformed into elaborate and playful objects when Gaudí and Jujol – Barcelona's leading architects – were responsible for their design. These bold mosaics represented a revival of a local tradition of ceramic decoration.

Orchestral innovator
(below) Pau Casals was a brilliant international cellist, deeply committed to the development of orchestral music in Barcelona. In 1920, he founded the Orquestra Pau Casals *which grew to dominate Barcelona's musical life until the end of the Spanish Civil War, attracting composers and conductors from all over the world.*

Archiv für Kunst und Geschichte

architectural debate and experimentation.

While every architect was searching for a new style to express both Barcelona's Catalan heritage and her modernity, views on the form it should take varied widely. The new architecture included buildings as diverse as the Palau de la Música Catalana, a flamboyant concert hall with a rather baroque appearance, encrusted with mosaics and sculpted decoration, and a number of imposing apartment blocks with the undulating contours and serpentine lines of Art Nouveau. As a young man, Dalí found these buildings particularly inspiring because of their 'irrational' quality. He was later to say that 'the ornamental shapes of Art Nouveau reveal to us in the most material way the persistence of dreams in the face of reality'.

ARCHITECTURAL REVIVAL

This fantasy element is nowhere more apparent than in the work of Barcelona's most celebrated architect, Antoni Gaudí. Like his contemporaries, Gaudí was eclectic in his approach, and he experimented with a number of stylistic elements derived from Gothic, Moorish and Baroque

Agenzia Zardoya

hidebound academic tradition, into a city with a lively awareness of the latest movements in European art. The artists Santiago Rusiñol, Ramon Casas and Miquel Utrillo had begun the trend when they went off to study in Paris in the 1890s. They haunted the famous nightclub, the Moulin de la Galette, from where they were able to observe at close quarters the bohemian enjoyments of Montmartre, which they did their best to recreate on their return to Spain. They also took back with them a lasting admiration for the work of the Impressionists, particularly Degas, and they followed the example he had set in painting the humble episodes of everyday life when they came to create their own distinctively Catalan version of Impressionist painting.

CAFÉ LIFE

Parisian café life also provided the inspiration behind the founding of Barcelona's first artistic café in 1897. Els Quatre Gats (The Four Cats) provided an essential meeting place for the town's progressive artists and intellectuals, and it mounted its own exhibitions, gave literary readings, and even produced its own magazine.

Arxiu Mas

traditions before he arrived at his own strikingly personal vision. His best-known works – the Parc Guell and the cathedral of the Sagrada Familia – are elaborate creations that are quite unlike anything that had been built before. Contemporaries were both enthralled and puzzled by the lofty towers and cavernous spaces of the Sagrada Familia, which is sometimes compared to a vast ruin or an oversize dovecote. For his part, Dalí saw in its organic, almost 'edible' forms, a premonition of the images of Surrealism.

Hand in hand with the architectural revival went a renewed interest in painting. By the turn of the century, Barcelona had transformed herself from an artistic backwater immersed in a

The Casa Milá
(above) Revealing Gaudí's unusual approach to urban architecture, the Casa Milà apartment block has been nicknamed 'the stone quarry'. Gaudí's love of ornate detail can be seen in the swirling shapes of the chimneys, and the intricate patterns of the balustrades – no two of which are cast in exactly the same design.

AISA

Poster art
(above) Strongly influenced by the ornate patterns of Art Nouveau, poster design in turn-of-the-century Barcelona developed into an art form in its own right.

Arxiu Mas

The modernista café
(left) Els Quatre Gats (The Four Cats) was the central meeting place for Barcelona's artists, musicians and poets. It produced its own art journal and exhibited work by the finest of the city's new painters.

Diaghilev's production of Eric Satie's *Parade,* for which Picasso, Miró and Cocteau designed the costumes and sets, was a sell-out.

Barcelona even supported its own Dada and Surrealist movements. Although shot in France, *Un Chien Andalou* (An Andalusian Dog), the outrageous film made by Dalí and Buñuel in 1928, noted for its mutilated eyeballs and rotting donkeys, took many of its ideas from the rich, imaginative Catalan background of the time. In 1932, work in a Surrealist vein received further encouragement when the *Amics de l'Art Nou* (Friends of the New Art) was founded, which aimed to promote any new and unusual developments in art. Besides putting on exhibitions of work by famous artists, the organisation staged shows of fairground objects, exhibitions of 'objects of bad taste', primitive art, children's art, and paintings by the insane.

Sadly, the period of liberalism and the great cultural renaissance that had lasted for almost half a century in Barcelona was brought to a brutal conclusion by the outbreak of civil war in 1936, and the reassertion of control by Madrid. But none were able to deny that Barcelona had established itself as the cultural capital of Spain.

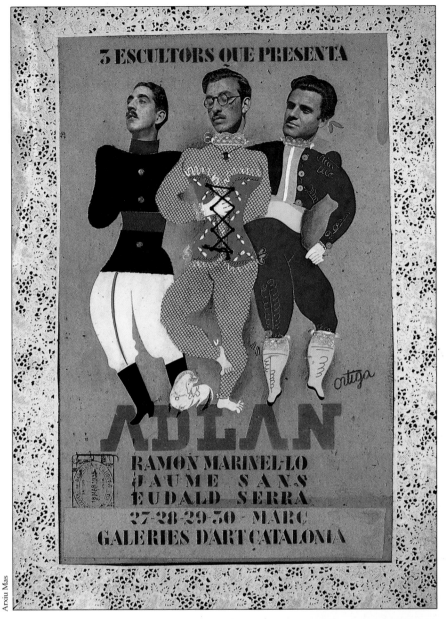

Arxiu Mas

Promoting Art

(left) Founded in 1932, ADLAN – Amics de l'Art Nou (Friends of New Art) – was an association designed to act as a forum and stimulus to avant-garde art or 'anything that is only supported by a select minority'. This collage poster advertises an exhibition by three surrealist painters who were contemporaries of Dalí.

Civil War

(below) With the outbreak of the Spanish Civil War in 1936, Barcelona's cultural renaissance came to an abrupt end. In this photograph, civilian volunteers join with Republican soldiers in preparation for the bloody struggle that was to cost Catalonia its political and artistic independence as Madrid, once again, assumed control.

Picasso became one of the café's regulars, and hung his paintings on its walls as the other painters did. He and his friends became Barcelona's second generation of avant-garde artists, who took artistic experimentation in the city several stages further, and who were not afraid to introduce social criticism into their work. Many of Picasso's paintings of the early 1900s, for instance, draw attention to lonely, underprivileged figures – those unable to share in Barcelona's new-found wealth.

Barcelona's neutrality during the First World War and the liberal attitude of its art establishment attracted several foreign artists to the city from 1916 onwards. They brought with them news of what was going on elsewhere in Europe, and helped popularize the work of the Cubists, Fauves and Futurists. Excitement about modern art was not just restricted to a small circle of connoisseurs. When Picasso returned to Barcelona from Paris in 1917, the city welcomed him back as a hero, and

Arxiu Mas

A Year in the Life 1975

Dalí, a self-proclaimed monarchist, had to wait until 1975 to see a king on the Spanish throne, the year America pulled out of Vietnam. Elsewhere, international terrorism reached epidemic proportions. In a year of such worldwide conflict the Apollo-Soyuz link-up was a rare display of peaceful co-operation.

On 20 November 1975 General Francisco Franco, victor of the Spanish Civil War, died after 36 years as El Caudillo (the Chief) of his new kingdom. Although, like Dalí, a professed monarchist, Franco had ruled as a dictator, while the monarchy remained in a strange state of suspended animation, with Prince Juan Carlos named as Franco's heir. Two days after the dictator's death he became king, and the membership of his first cabinet suggested that he might not be completely hostile to reform. In the event, Juan Carlos I was to engineer a complete break with the Franco régime.

The United States ended her painful 15-year involvement with Vietnam as the Communist North Vietnamese and Viet Cong swept to victory. After 57,000 American deaths, 150,000 serious casualties, and savage bombings of the North that had

NASA

Detente in space

(left) On 17 July 1975, a Soviet Soyuz space vehicle docked in space with an American Apollo capsule. The specially constructed docking module (DM) on the Apollo craft contained life support systems and a communications link to connect the two space vehicles. The DM is seen here in part as American astronaut Slayton and a Soviet cosmonaut pose with a certain amount of difficulty for the NASA cameras. After two days of joint operations which included experimentation with higher temperature crystallisation, and crew members' visits to each other's spacefraft, the vehicles separated and re-docked to separate once again. This co-operative mission was the final flight of an Apollo spacecraft.

Science Photo Library

India in ferment

(right) In 1971, nine million Bengali refugees fled into India from East Pakistan. Although they were soon to form the new state of Bangladesh, this drain on India's financial resources combined with the OPEC oil price rise of 1973 and rapid population growth led to increasing political unrest. In June 1975, the Prime Minister, Mrs Indira Gandhi, despite her conviction for technical electoral violations, declared a state of emergency which was to last until March 1977. Opposition leaders were imprisoned, censorship was imposed and central government acquired control of the judiciary and state government. Mrs Gandhi also initiated the notorious birth control campaign which resulted in the sterilization of nearly 11 million people.

K. Chawla/The Hutchinson Library

angered much world opinion, the United States had withdrawn most of her troops. However, several thousand remained behind in an effort to make the army of the South efficient enough to defend itself. The policy was a complete failure. In December 1974, the Communist forces launched an offensive and, as Phuoc Long, Da Nang and Hue fell in rapid succession, the Americans began to move tens of thousands of South Vietnamese who feared they would suffer from their association with the collapsing régime. On 29 April, with Northern forces approaching the capital from five directions, American Service Radio in Saigon played 'I'm dreaming of a White Christmas' and broadcast the fake weather forecast 'it's 105 degrees rising' – the signal to quit. One helicopter after another landed in the courtyard or on the roof of the US embassy, then took off crammed with Americans and the luckier Vietnamese. Meanwhile thousands of the not-so-lucky besieged the embassy, and there were harrowing scenes as they were fought off by the Marines. The last Americans left Vietnam at 7.53 am on 30 April. By noon Saigon had been completely occupied and the war was over.

WAVE OF INTERNATIONAL TERRORISM

Terrorism was constantly in the news, and seemed to be reaching epidemic proportions. In 1975 there were IRA bombings and shootings in England and Ireland; Arab terrorists committed outrages at Orly airport, Tel Aviv, Jerusalem and even Vienna, where 11 OPEC oil ministers were

Nik Wheeler/Black Star/Colorific

Saigon evacuated
(left) In 1975, America's ten-year war against communism in South Vietnam finally ended. Early in the year, former President Nixon's boast of 'Peace with honour' seemed hollow as the US decision to evacuate led to the collapse of the Thieu government of South Vietnam while North Vietnamese forces pushed down to Saigon. The final airlift took place within the US Embassy grounds in Saigon on 30 April – a massive 18-hour operation that carried 1373 Americans and nearly 6000 Vietnamese out of the country to safety. Thousands of the less fortunate swarmed the Embassy walls.

Popperfoto

Tragic assassination
(right) King Feisal ibn Abdul Aziz of Saudi Arabia was shot dead by a nephew on 25 March 1975. A powerful and greatly respected leader, King Feisal had had the doubly difficult task of transforming his oil-rich kingdom into a modern state while at the same time working hard for Arab unity.

held as hostages; the Baader-Meinhof gang was active in West Germany; two attempts were made to assassinate the American President Ford; and in Holland, South Moluccans hijacked a train and held out for 8 days.

There were many other headline-making events in 1975. This was International Women's Year, and fittingly, one member of a 15-woman Japanese expedition became the first of her sex to reach the summit of Mount Everest. In the United States, the principal White House defendants in the Watergate affair (which had brought down President Nixon the previous year) were gaoled. So were 'the Colonels' whose junta had ruled over Greece from 1967 to 1974. The American heiress Pattie Hearst, who had been kidnapped by urban guerrillas and had apparently joined them, was located and arrested. With a

Soviet-American *detente* in the making, the Soyuz 19 and Apollo 15 spacecraft docked in outer space, and the crews exchanged visits. In India, Mrs Gandhi reacted to charges of corruption and legal disqualification from politics by arresting hundreds of her political opponents. Newly independent Bangladesh elected popular hero Sheik Mujibur Rahman as its first president, but by August he had become widely enough disliked to be murdered in the course of a military coup. Finally, in Britain the first-ever referendum determined that Britain would stay in the Common Market; in June, the first North Sea oil was pumped from the Argyll field off the Scottish coast; legal efforts to prevent publication of Labour cabinet minister Richard Crossman's diaries failed; and Mrs Margaret Thatcher was elected leader of the Conservative Party.

Mary Fisher/Colorific

Haldemann before the Watergate Committee

(above) At the end of May 1972, a group of former CIA agents broke into the Democratic Party headquarters at the Watergate Hotel in Washington during the Presidential election campaign. This unconstitutional action, organised by White House aides, was followed up by the 'break-in' of 17 June when the agents were caught red-handed with bugging and photographic equipment. For the next six months, the White House led by Nixon's chief of staff, Bob Haldemann, made every effort to cover up the affair by intimidation, bribery and suppression of evidence to conceal the extraordinary corruption that had accompanied Nixon's re-election campaign. Hearings by a Senate Select Committee began the next year. The President's claim to ignorance of the affair was belied by the eventual surrender of White House tapes discussing Watergate strategy and he resigned on 8 August 1974. The hearings continued until the following January, when Haldemann and three colleagues were indicted.

Popperfoto

From dictatorship to monarchy

(left) General Francisco Franco of Spain is seen here with his designated successor, the Bourbon Prince Juan Carlos. In the late autumn of 1975, the 82-year-old dictator became critically ill and was obliged to hand over power to his heir on 30 October, thus marking an end to his 36-year-old régime. He died three weeks later. On 22 November, Juan Carlos took his oath as the new King of Spain.

GALLERY GUIDE

Rousseau
Rousseau is best-known for his exotic jungle scenes and fine examples of these can be seen in Paris (p.31), London (pp.24-5) and, in America, at galleries in Washington (p.21), New York (pp.34-5) and Philadelphia (p.30). The best general collections of his work are in Paris and New York. The former possesses samples of his portraiture at the Louvre and at the Musée d'Orsay. Two of his most striking canvases are in New York, at the Museum of Modern Art (pp.28-9) and at the Guggenheim Museum (p.32), while the Mellon Collection houses one of his many Parisian views and a remarkable still-life. Rousseau's work can also be found at the Pushkin Museum in Moscow.

Klee
The largest collection of the artist's work is to be found in the Paul Klee Foundation in Berne. Further examples are featured in the city's own gallery and in the collections at Basel and Lucerne. Outside his native Switzerland, Klee is best-represented in Germany. The Kunstsammlung Nordrhein-Westfalen, at Düsseldorf, owns a charming souvenir of his Tunisian trip (*Red and White Cupolas*) and the supremely witty *Black Prince*. Munich (p.58) and Essen (*Fire by Full Moon*) also contain excellent examples of his work. In America, Klee's major paintings can be seen in New York, Philadelphia and Washington.

Chagall
Chagall is strongly represented in the United States. At the Guggenheim Museum, in New York, there is one of the finest of his many portrayals of musicians. Chicago owns *The White Crucifixion*, while in Philadelphia and St Louis there are superb examples of his Cubist phase. The Museum of Modern Art, New York, houses the delightful portrait of the artist with his wife (pp.90-91) and there are variants on this theme in Leningrad and Paris. In Europe, the best collections are in Amsterdam and in Paris and there is a Chagall Museum at Cimiez, near Nice. The artist's Jewish roots are reflected in many of his paintings; the outstanding example (pp.94-5) is owned by the Tel-Aviv Museum, and there are further excellent works on this subject in Venice, Düsseldorf and Leningrad. Late in his career, Chagall became involved with the decorative arts and his greatest achievements in this field were the stained glass windows for the Hadassah University Medical Centre, in Jerusalem (pp.98-9), and his ceiling for the Paris Opéra.

Dalí
There are two specialist collections devoted to Dalí's work, one at his birthplace, Figueras and the other at St Petersburg, Florida. Other American galleries are also rich in Dalí's work, the most striking examples being in New York (pp.120-21), Philadelphia (*Soft Construction with Boiled Beans . . .*) and Hartford, Connecticut (*Apparition of Face and Fruit Dish on a Beach*). The best selections of Dalí's early pictures are to be found in Barcelona and Madrid (p.118), while his mature style is particularly well-represented in Rotterdam. In Britain, the Glasgow Art Gallery contains the finest example of the artist's startling religious imagery, while his obsessive sexual interests can be viewed in Stockholm (*The Enigma of William Tell*), Lugano (*Dream caused by the Flight of a Bee . . .*) and Zurich (*The Enigma of Desire*). Much of Dalí's work remains in private hands.

BIBLIOGRAPHY

D. Ades, *Dada and Surrealism*, Barron, Eaglewood Cliffs, 1978
S. Alexandrian, *Surrealist Art*, Thames and Hudson, New York, 1985
D. Chevalier, *Klee*, Crown, New York, 1983
R. Cogniat, *Chagall*, Crown, New York, 1983
R. Descharnes, *Dalí*, Abrams, New York, 1985
C. Giedon-Welcker, *Paul Klee*, Lund Humphries, Bradford, 1954
W. Haftman, *Chagall*, Abrams, New York, 1984
A. Jakovsky, *Naive Painting*, Phaidon, Oxford, 1979

F. Klee, *The Diaries of Paul Klee, 1898-1918*, University of California, Berkeley, 1964
J. Pierre, *Surrealism*, Barron, New York, 1979
U. Schneede, *Surrealism*, Abrams, New York, 1973
R. Short, *Paul Klee*, Thames and Hudson, London, 1979
C. Sorlier (ed.), *Chagall by Chagall*, Adams, New York, 1979
D. Vallier, *Henri Rousseau*, Crown, New York, 1979
P. Waldberg, *Le Surréalisme*, Skire, Geneva, 1962
S. Wilson, *Surrealist Painting*, Salem House, Eaglewood Cliffs, 1983

Wilhelm Lehmbruch Museum, Duisberg/© DACS 1988

Hans Bellmer (b.1902)

Surrealist painter, draughtsman and sculptor. Born in Katowice, in Silesia, Bellmer studied in Berlin, initially with the intention of becoming an engineer, like his father. However, the Dadaist works of Grosz and Dix led him to abandon this course and he started earning his living as an illustrator. Bellmer's links with Surrealism began after his trips to Paris in the 1920s and he eventually settled there in 1938. His favourite image was that of the doll – a popular Surrealist theme – and after 1933 this motif dominated all aspects of his work. In sculpture, he produced several versions of a figure with two pairs of legs, attached to either side of a central 'stomach ball', and his distortions of female anatomy were repeated in elegant but disturbing graphic works.

Camille Bombois (1883-1970)

After Rousseau, the best-known French Naive painter. Bombois came from a rural background and was largely self-taught. For many years, he was an amateur artist, working by day and painting by night. The most enduring of his many day-jobs was as a compositor, but it was his period as a circus wrestler that had the greatest effect on his art, inspiring numerous pictures on this theme. In 1928, Bombois' work was exhibited alongside that of Rousseau, and in the latter part of his career his miniatures brought him considerable financial success.

Giorgio de Chirico (1888-1978)

Italian Metaphysical painter. De Chirico was born in Greece but trained in Munich, where his main influences were the Symbolist works of Klinger and Böcklin. He

Surreal temptation
(above) In The Temptation of St Anthony *(1945), Max Ernst explores a theme popular with medieval artists like Hieronymus Bosch, whose fantastic visions of Hell led Surrealists like Ernst to regard him as a precursor of their movement.*

travelled in Italy during 1909-10 and it was here that he found the inspiration for his earliest 'metaphysical' paintings – disquieting urban landscapes, inhabited only by statues or mannequins and enveloped in a pervasive air of melancholy. From 1911-15, de Chirico was in Paris, where he exhibited with the avant-garde at the Salon d'Automne, but he was really only understood by Picasso and Apollinaire. During the war years, he was posted to Ferrara where, with the Futurist artist Carlo Carrà, he invented pittura metafisica *(metaphysical painting). This short-lived movement, with its emphasis on the juxtaposition of incompatible objects, was to create an important precedent for the Surrealists. However, de Chirico quarrelled with Carrà in 1919 and, by the time Surrealism was properly launched, he was working in a much more traditional vein.*

Paul Delvaux (b.1897)

Belgian Surrealist painter. Delvaux trained as an architect in Brussels and painted briefly in the Neo-Impressionist and Expressionist styles. However, in 1934 his imagination was fired by an exhibition of the works of Magritte and de Chirico and he turned to Surrealism. His pictures combined elements from both these artists, marrying the startling clarity of the former with de Chirico's lonely cityscapes. Delvaux's own store of imagery was enriched by a trip to Italy in 1939, which reawakened his interest in Roman architecture and classical nudes. However, his most distinctive creation was la ville inquiète *(the uneasy city), a mysterious, environment, usually depicted at night and inhabited only by skeletons, trains and erotic nudes.*

Max Ernst (1891-1976)

German painter; the most varied and inventive of the Surrealists. Ernst studied philosophy at Bonn and was introduced to painting by August Macke, a member of the Blaue Reiter *group. After World War One, he helped found the Dada movement in Cologne and began experimenting with collages. In 1922, he arrived in Paris, where his style soon reflected the vogue for de Chirico's dream-like compositions. Ernst was a founder member of the Surrealist group and remained loyal to it until 1938, when an argument with Breton obliged him to leave the movement. His own work during this period showed a remarkable versatility and a willingness to explore new techniques. The most notable of these were his* frottages *('rubbings' used in conjunction with automatic drawing) and his use of decalcomania (a transfer process involving gouache paints). Ernst was forced to flee to America in 1941, where he produced a series of fantastic landscapes, symbolizing the devastations of war. He returned to France in 1953.*

Morris Hirschfield (1872-1946)

Leading American Naive painter. Hirschfield was born in Poland and emigrated to the USA in 1890. He worked in a ladies' fashion house and set up his own shoe factory, only turning to painting late in life, when ill-health had forced him to retire from business. Hirschfield's taste was for ornamental scenes of female nudes, surrounded by flowers or animals, and his pictures appealed to the Surrealists because of their remarkable blend of ingenuousness and fetishism.

Mikhail Fedorovich Larionov (1881-1964)

Russian Modernist painter, the inventor of Rayonnism. Larionov trained in Moscow, where he met his lifelong companion and fellow artist, Natalia Goncharova (1881-1962). Together, they were at the forefront of the Russian avant-garde experiments and exhibited in Paris, at the Salon d'Automne. Larionov was a founder member of the 'Knave of Diamonds', a short-lived exhibiting group which introduced the latest European trends to Moscow, and, in 1912, he was invited to show with the Blaue Reiter *in Munich. At this period, his art had much in common with that of Chagall, both men working in a neo-primitive style that drew heavily on Russian folk imagery. In 1913, Larionov published his Rayonnist manifesto, which blended Russian nationalism with Futurist elements, but the outbreak of war interrupted his artistic development. In 1915, both he and Goncharova left Russia permanently.*

René Magritte (1898-1967)

Leading Belgian Surrealist painter. Magritte studied at the Académie des Beaux-Arts in Brussels and his earliest pictures were mostly Abstract or Cubist in style. However, in 1922, he was deeply impressed by de Chirico's Song of Love *and this drew him towards the Surrealist movement – a tendency that was reinforced during his stay in Paris (1927-30), when he was in close contact with Breton, Ernst and Eluard. Magritte's main concern was with the paradoxical and, accordingly, many of his canvases took the form of semantic jokes. In common with Delvaux, he employed a meticulous, illusionistic technique to make the ambiguities in his* work appear even more startling to the spectator. This dream-like clarity was later to inspire Pop artists such as Jim Dine and Claes Thure Oldenburg.*

André Masson (1896-1988)

French painter, briefly associated with the Surrealists. Masson settled in Paris in 1920, meeting Miró the following year. His early taste for Cubism was modified by experiments with automatic drawing. In 1924, his first one-man exhibition attracted the attention of Breton, who invited him to join the Surrealist movement. Masson's association with the group was short-lived, as he quarrelled with the autocratic Breton in 1929. During this time, however, he pioneered the development of automatic art through his sand paintings. These were created from the random patterns which the artist obtained by pouring sand over glue-covered canvases.

Pierre Roy (1880-1950)

French painter and designer, associated with the Surrealists. Roy was born in Nantes but trained in Paris, where his first enthusiasm was for Fauvist art. In 1919, he met de Chirico and, through him, came into contact with Max Ernst and the Surrealist poets. Roy contributed to the first exhibition of the group in 1925, but was never deeply committed to the movement. However, his taste for producing strange and menacing juxtapositions of objects was typical of the earliest phase of Surrealism. The best-known of these is Danger on the Stairs *(c.1928, Museum of Modern Art, New York), where a large snake slithers down a staircase.*

Yves Tanguy (1900-55)

French Surrealist painter. Tanguy's father had been a sea-captain and, accordingly, Yves began his working life as a merchant seaman. However, after seeing a de Chirico painting in a dealer's window, he decided abruptly to turn to art. His early pictures (most of which he later destroyed) were in the naive style of Rousseau but, by the mid 1920s, Tanguy had moved on to more traditional Surrealist territory and was experimenting with automatic paintings. These rapidly evolved into the visionary landscapes which were the trademark of his maturity. Tanguy's landscapes were probably inspired by the strange rock formations which he had witnessed during boyhood trips to Brittany and he peopled them with melting, biomorphic forms that were reminiscent of those portrayed by Miró and Dalí. He married the American painter, Kay Sage, and settled in the USA, becoming a naturalized citizen in 1948.

Dorothea Tanning (b.1912)

American Surrealist painter, born in Galesburg, Illinois. Tanning trained briefly at the Chicago Academy of Arts, but left for New York in 1935. In the following year, a major exhibition of Dada and Surrealist art at the Museum of Modern Art drew her to the movement and this direction was confirmed after her meeting with Max Ernst in 1942. Tanning married Ernst in 1946 and the couple moved to Sedona, Arizona. In 1944, her first one-woman show was held in New York, at the Julien Levy Gallery. Tanning's pictures usually depict pubescent girls in bizarre or horrifying situations, and there is frequently a strong sexual undercurrent.

INDEX